THE LEGEND
OF THE
MASTER

THE LEGEND
OF THE
MASTER

❖

HENRY JAMES

Compiled by
SIMON NOWELL-SMITH

JAMES, HENRY, O.M. 1843–1916 — Of
American birth; novelist of the experiences of the
cultivated mind; famous for his conversation.
Catalogue of the National Portrait Gallery

But after all I have been led into trying to present
Henry James dramatically, and that is to invite
disaster. *Compton Mackenzie*

Oxford   New York
OXFORD UNIVERSITY PRESS
1985

Oxford University Press, Walton Street, Oxford OX2 6DP

Oxford New York Toronto
Delhi Bombay Calcutta Madras Karachi
Kuala Lumpur Singapore Hong Kong Tokyo
Nairobi Dar es Salaam Cape Town
Melbourne Auckland

and associated companies in
Beirut Berlin Ibadan Nicosia

Oxford is a trade mark of Oxford University Press

First published 1947 by Constable and Company
First issued as an Oxford University Press paperback 1985

British Library Cataloguing in Publication Data

The legend of the master: Henry James.
1. James, Henry. 1843–1916——Biography
2. Novelists, America——Biography
I. Nowell-Smith, Simon
813'.4 PS2123

ISBN 0-19-281921-6

Library of Congress Cataloging in Publication Data

Nowell-Smith, Simon, 1909–
The legend of the master, Henry James.
Reprint. Originally published: London:
Constable, 1947.
Bibliography: p. Includes index.
1. James, Henry, 1843–1916——Biography——Addresses,
essays, lectures. 2. Novelists, American——19th
century——Biography——Addresses, essays, lectures.
I. Title.
PS2123.N6 1985 813'.4 [B] 85-15550

ISBN 0-19-281921-6 (pbk).

Set by Colset Private Ltd.
Printed in Great Britain by
Richard Clay (The Chaucer Press) Ltd.
Bungay, Suffolk

CONTENTS

For MARION
(my wife till her death in 1977)
1947

For LEON
(trusted mentor and loved friend since 1947)
1985

CHRONOLOGICAL TABLE

Life

1843 Born 15 April in New York, second son of Henry James, theologian. (The first son was William James the philosopher.)

1843-4 First visit to Europe.

1845-55 Lives in Albany, NY, and New York City. A succession of governesses and day schools.

1855-60 Mainly spent in Switzerland, England, France and Germany, with innumerable changes of governess, tutor and school. Real education derived from unrestricted access to books, galleries and theatres.

1860-2 Lives in Newport, RI. Attends studio of William Morris Hunt.

1862 Spends a year at Harvard Law School at Cambridge, Mass.

1864 James family move to Boston, and later (1866) to Cambridge. Friendship with W. D. Howells begun.

1869-70 Visits England and Switzerland, makes extensive tour of Italy. Imbibes 'European virus'. Death of his cousin Minnie Temple. Returns to America.

1872-4 With commission to write travel articles visits England, Switzerland, Bavaria, Low Countries; stays in Paris, Rome and Florence. Friendship with J. R. Lowell. Interest in French theatre develops. Returns to America.

1875 Decides to settle in Europe. Lives in Paris. Friendship

Writings

Note. — Important works only are listed. Dates in parentheses refer to first book publication.

c.1853 Begins writing and illustrating plays (or at least scenes: 'I am not positively certain I arrived at acts').

1860 Writes Tennysonian verse.

1864 First contribution to an American periodical.

1865-78 JOURNALISM. — Frequent book and theatre reviews, art criticisms, travel articles and short stories. After 1878 the volume of journalism declines.

1871 Publication of 'A Passionate Pilgrim', earliest magazine story which James later thought worth reprinting.

1874 Writes first full-length novel (*Roderick Hudson*).

1875-89 FIRST FICTION PERIOD

Novels: *Roderick Hudson* (1876); *The American* (1877); *The Europeans* (1878); *Confidence* (1880); *The Portrait of a Lady* (1881); *The Bostonians* (1886); *The Princess*

Life

with Turgenev, Flaubert, Daudet, Maupassant, Zola.

1876–81 Settles in London. Frequent visits to the Continent. Serial publication of *Daisy Miller* (1878) brings entrée into London literary and social circles. Becomes an assiduous diner-out.

1881–2 Visits America as successful novelist. Mother dies. First play (*Daisy Miller*) rejected in New York and London.

1882 Tours Touraine and Provence. Friendship with George du Maurier and Edmund Gosse begun. Father dies.

1882–3 Again visits America. Returns to life in London.

1885 Alice James arrives as an invalid in England. Friendship with R. L. Stevenson and Sidney Colvin. Stays at Broadway with colony of artists including Sargent, Abbey and Alfred Parsons.

1886–7 Extended visit to Italy. Shorter continental visits continue for several years.

1889–95 Moves much in theatrical circles. Of several plays written, only *The American* (1891) and *Guy Domville* (1895) are produced. Friendships with Elizabeth Robins, Arthur Benson and Logan Pearsall Smith begun.

1892 Alice James dies.

1894 Stevenson dies.

1895 The Daudets visit London.

1896 Stays at Rye, sees Lamb House.

1897 Rents (later buys) Lamb House. Thereafter spends most summers in Rye and winters in London. Sussex friends include Conrad and H. G. Wells.

Writings

Casamassima (1886); *The Reverberator* (1888)

Stories: *A Passionate Pilgrim* (1875); *Watch and Ward* (1878); *Daisy Miller* (1879); *The Madonna of the Future* (1879); *Washington Square* (1881); *The Siege of London* (1883); *Tales of Three Cities* (1884); *Stories Revived* (1885); *The Aspern Papers* (1888); *A London Life* (1889)

Other books: *Transatlantic Sketches* (1875); *French Poets and Novelists* (1878); *Hawthorne* (1879); *Portraits of Places* (1883); *A Little Tour in France* (1885); *Partial Portraits* (1888)

1890–1900 SECOND FICTION PERIOD

Novels: *The Tragic Muse* (1890); *The Other House* (1896); *The Spoils of Poynton* (1897); *What Maisie Knew* (1897); *In the Cage* (1898); *The Awkward Age* (1899)

Stories: *The Lesson of the Master* (1892); *The Private Life* (1893); *The Real Thing* (1893); *Terminations* (1895); *Embarrassments* (1896); *The Two Magics* (1898); *The Soft Side* (1900)

Plays: *Theatricals, I* (1894); *Theatricals, II* (1895)

Other books: *Picture and Text* (1893); *Essays in London* (1893)

Life

1904–5 With commission for travel book pays first visit for 20 years to America, going for first time to California. Elected to American Academy of Letters and Arts. Delivers lectures in Philadelphia and elsewhere.

1906–8 Revises novels and stories for collected edition with new critical prefaces.

1907 Inspired by repertory movement returns to play-writing. *The High Bid* (1908) and *The Saloon* (1911) produced.

1909 Friendship with Rupert Brooke and Hugh Walpole begun. Seriously ill in winter of 1909–10

1910–11 Final visit to America. William James dies. Awarded honorary degree at Harvard.

1912 Awarded honorary D. Litt. (*fecundissimus et facundissimus scriptor*) at Oxford. Delivers Browning centenary address before Academic Committee of Royal Society of Literature.

1913 Painted by Sargent in celebration of 70th birthday.

1914 With outbreak of war moves to London; works for American ambulance corps, Belgian refugees and other causes.

1915 Naturalized as British subject, 26 July.

1916 Awarded Order of Merit, January. Dies 28 February. Ashes buried in Cambridge, Mass.

Writings

THIRD FICTION PERIOD

Novels: *The Sacred Fount* (1901); *The Wings of the Dove* (1902); *The Ambassadors* (1903); *The Golden Bowl* (1904); *The Outcry* (1911)

Stories: *The Better Sort* (1903); *The Finer Grain* (1910)

Criticism: Prefaces to collected *Novels and Tales* (1908–9)

Other books: *William Wetmore Story* (1903); *English Hours* (1905); *The American Scene* (1907); *Italian Hours* (1909)

1913–15 LAST WRITINGS

Reminiscence: *A Small Boy and Others* (1913); *Notes of a Son and Brother* (1914); *The Middle Years* (1917, unfinished)

Criticism: *Notes on Novelists* (1914)

Novels: *The Ivory Tower* (1917, unfinished); *The Sense of the Past* (1917, unfinished)

War essays: *Within the Rim* (1918)

THE LEGEND

A quite legendary figure, a sort of stuffed waxwork from whose mouth a stream of coloured sentences, like winding rolls of green and pink paper, are for ever issuing.

The figure is Henry James's and the words are Hugh Walpole's. Several factors helped, in Walpole's view, to create this popular and false image. There were the elaborate prefaces to the collected *Novels and Tales*; there were the published letters — voluminous, mannered and to the casual reader wearisome and seemingly insincere; there was the 'quarrel with Wells'; and there were anecdotes told by those who had scarcely known the Master. The published letters may be safely left, to all but the most casual reader, to speak for themselves of James's wisdom and his foibles, his conventionalities and idiosyncrasies, his tendernesses and his often disconcerting sincerities. Of the relations between James and H. G. Wells the discerning reader may judge by reading the letters that they exchanged after the publication of *Boon* in 1915 and by observing that Wells in his autobiography passed the matter over in silence. But what of the anecdotes? Mrs Wharton declares that James's letters, delightful as they are, give only hints and fragments of his talk; and more than one of his friends have deplored that no recording Boswell was at hand. Was this talk a stream of coloured sentences for ever issuing from the mouth of a stuffed waxwork? Had James, as Thomas Hardy wrote in his diary, a ponderously warm manner of saying nothing in infinite sentences? Or were Anstey and Alfred Sutro right in asserting that if he took his time he always finally reached a point that was well worth waiting for? Was James in old age, as someone described him to Stephen Spender, a frozen-up old monster? or were courtesy, kindness and humour,

as Mrs Paul Draper averred, the high lights that played upon the
surface of a profound wisdom and intellectual clarity?

This book arose in the first place from a suspicion that some of
the familiar stories about James and sayings ascribed to him
might be apocryphal, and from an attempt to trace suspicious
anecdotes to contemporary sources. Just as Dr Spooner's
idiosyncrasy of speech led many spurious spoonerisms to be
fathered upon him; just as, during their lives and long after their
deaths, any sufficiently epigrammatic witticism was apt to be
attributed to Whistler or Wilde, or both — so, it seemed possible,
Jacobesque phrases of familiar form and polish might have been
passed off as genuine Jacobean. Not every raconteur with a good
story to tell will candidly preface it, as G. K. Chesterton did one
story of James, with the words, 'The legend says (I never learned
for certain if it was true) . . .'; or round it off, as Miss Jordan did
another, with 'I never believed that one.' When Joseph Pennell
wrote that James had described certain visitors to Rye as 'sad
wantons, one of whom was not without a pale cadaverous
grace' — the earliest printed record (1925) that I know of this *mot*
in more or less its accepted form — several questions arose. Did
Pennell hear James say this? Did William Rothenstein, who
quoted the words slightly differently six years later? Neither
claims to have done so, but if they did not, then did James in fact
say anything of the sort? or was it the phrase-making of another,
too good and too characteristically Jacobean to be lost in the
limbo of anonymity? Even with apparently well-attested anecdotes it seemed possible that James's peculiar mode of speech
might have stimulated the imaginative invention alike of those
who had scarcely known him and of others whose memory for
detail was defective. For epigram apart — and he had a reputation
for epigram in the 'eighties — that speech in later years took the
form of 'infinite sentences', 'impassioned soliloquies', 'a sort of
Chinese nest of parentheses'. If Arthur Benson, committing a
soliloquy to his diary on the evening after it had been delivered,
found it wise to add, 'I think I have got this marvellous tirade
nearly correct', who, recording after ten or twenty or thirty
years 'the slow accumulation of detail, the widening sweep, the

interjection of grotesque and emphatic images, the studied exaggerations', the *motif* 'precisely enunciated, revised, elongated, improved upon, enriched', could honestly claim that the record was true? Who moreover might not have fallen into the temptation to miniate a text which — without the 'rich and flexible' tones of the Master, the 'delicious gesture, the upturned eye, the clenched upheld hand', 'the jolly laughter' or the 'stony twinkle of innocent malice' — must seem lacking in colour?

Before 1916, with perhaps the single exception of Wells's *Boon*, there were no printed sources for the legend in its extreme form. Parodies of the 'third manner' of writing there were in plenty; there were one or two recognizable but inoffensive portraits in fiction; but courtesy forbade all save his friend Wells to combine criticism of James's writing with caricature of his speech in a manner calculated to wound. (Wells acknowledged later that *Boon* had been a retaliation for the way in which James, in *Notes on Novelists*, had put him 'in a bundle with a company of young men of questionable quality as one of the Younger Reputations'.) The tradition thus far was oral, so that the search into its origins had to be limited almost wholly to books of autobiography and recollection published since 1916. Here was a wealth of material: of positive value if the books contained letters or diaries written at the time of the events recorded, of more doubtful value if the records were mere unattested reminiscence.

There is in E. F. Benson's *Final Edition* a warning to writers of books of autobiography and reminiscence. It is both generally and particularly apt to the present inquiry.

As I thought over various very entertaining volumes of the sort which I had recently read, it appeared to me that not only had their writers retained their recollective powers in the most amazing manner, but that some of them had brought up, as an unnecessary reinforcement to memory, imaginations of the most magical kind. Not only did they remember and record interesting experiences which had never happened to themselves, but experiences which had never happened to anybody.

Benson gave examples, convincing examples narrated with sympathetic irony, and went on:

Readers then may properly demand of autobiographical authors that they should depend on their memory or their documents, and that when memory fails as they struggle to push their way along the overgrown paths of the past they must make sure that an imprudent step on to an attractive patch of vivid green should not land them in a bog-hole. In setting their scene no one will grudge them a reasonable licence in decoration in order to adorn what would otherwise be a bald narrative. But caution is required.

He then quoted from a recent book a description of James's house at Rye as 'majestic', of its lawn as 'immense', and of its garden walls as of 'grey stone': in fact Lamb House, as Benson, himself for many years a tenant, pointed out (with more irony), though of a modest dignity, is decidedly small, its lawn is not large enough for an averagely energetic game of tennis and its garden is surrounded by walls of red brick. Such inaccuracies may seem trivial enough. Yet they assume some importance when it comes to assessing the testimony of those who fostered the legend. If the writer in question — F. M. Hueffer in *Return to Yesterday* — was so unobservant a painter of landscape, are his interiors any more to be trusted? Or his portraits? Or his conversation pieces?

Benson was a first-rate anecdotist. Over twenty years he wrote a number of books of family history and personal reminiscence. Each read singly is rewarding, but read in sequence they appear remarkably, even tediously repetitive. James once told Benson's mother that his early work had been 'subaqueous': Benson tell us this in *Our Family Affairs* (1920), in *As We Were* (1930), in his Introduction to James's letters to Arthur Benson (1930) and in *Final Edition* (1940). In the same four books he quotes selected phrases from two letters which James wrote to him about *Dodo*; in two of the four books he recapitulates, and in a third alludes to, one of James's impassioned soliloquies delivered in his presence in the garden of Lamb House; in two he records James's periphrasis for 'black dog'. Now these repetitions would not matter, would suggest no more than a dearth of copy for a new book, were they consistent. But not all of them are. One of the *Dodo* letters is first given at some length, to all appearance transcribed from the original; one passage reads: 'For the rest, make yourself a style. It is by style we are saved.' Ten years later, isolated from the rest of the letter and presumably quoted from memory, this has become: 'Hew out a style . . .' — a *varia lectio* which ten years later again has become the received text. 'Readers then may properly demand of autobiographical authors that they should depend on . . . their documents.' Similarly the soliloquy at Rye is once given in direct speech, only to be broken off with the admission that there were other 'picturesque phrases which I can no longer recapture'; in the second version it is abridged and paraphrased, but one or two of the missing phrases have meanwhile been recaptured. It is difficult to avoid the suspicion that this first-rate anecdotist had thought up one or two 'good ones' in the interval. 'They must make sure that an imprudent step on to an attractive patch of vivid green should not land them in a bog-hole.'

Five years after Pennell in *The Adventures of an Illustrator* had conjured up James's cadaverous wanton E. F. Benson published his *As We Were*. There he told the story — or a story — at considerable length:

. . . the story of the two nimble and fashionable dames who had a thirst for the capture of celebrities. Both longed to add Henry James to their collections, and having ascertained that he was at Rye, they travelled down from London, rang the bell at Lamb House, and sent in their cards. He did not much relish these ruthless methods but, after all, they were in earnest, for they had come far in pursuit, and with much courtesy he shewed them his house, refreshed them with tea, and took them for a stroll through the picturesque little town, guiding them to the church and the gun-garden, and the Ypres tower and the Elizabethan inn. The appearance of these two brilliant strangers in his company naturally aroused a deal of pleasant interest among his friends in Rye, and next day one of them called on him, bursting with laudable curiosity to know who these dazzling creatures were. She made an arch and pointed allusion to the two pretty ladies with whom she had seen him yesterday.

'Yes,' he said, 'I believe, indeed I noticed, that there were some faint traces of bygone beauty on the face of one of the two poor wantons.'

In support of his story Benson says that it was told him in that form at least a couple of years later; that he thereupon repeated it at a luncheon party to one of the most enterprising hostesses in London, who was not amused but abruptly changed the subject;

and that a friend after lunch asked him, 'What on earth possessed you to tell her that? Don't you know that she was one of them?'

This seemed circumstantial enough — the smart celebrity-hunters; the journey from London; the unheralded arrival at Lamb House; the perambulation of Rye; the arch and inquisitive local inhabitant; the Master's *mot* (a little more diffuse than one might have wished, but surely the *ipsissima verba*); and finally two years later the embarrassing anagnorisis. And yet . . . Benson after all had not been present at Rye; that part, the essential part, of the story he had by his own admission only on hearsay, and the account of the occasion as given to him two years later might have been distorted. His only supporting evidence is that the hostess to whom he retailed it recognized herself, or rather was assumed by Benson's other friend to have recognized herself, as a protagonist. Perhaps — it seems at first sight far-fetched — the hostess had been over-sensitive in wearing a cap that fitted some other occasion; perhaps even she had other, now irrecoverable grounds for her abrupt change of subject.

Some such hypothesis — assuming that Benson was too prudent to record 'experiences which had never happened to anybody' — is clearly required by the evidence. For a year after Benson's book was published there appeared Evan Charteris's life of Edmund Gosse, and in it a letter of 20 November 1899 to Maurice Baring (quoted on page 115 below): the letter was written within a few days, if not a few hours, of the utterance of the *mot*, and it says that according to James some young actresses (not fashionable dames), staying at Winchelsea (not in London), had at their expressed desire (not unheralded) gone to Lamb House to tea. No picturesque details about the picturesque tour of the town; no local female friend with laudable curiosity and arch allusions; but Gosse in person to ask whether the visitors had been pretty. And the reply — pithier than in Benson's version yet without the litotes (just such a Jacobesque embellishment as oral tradition might be expected to add) of Pennell's: 'He replied, "Pretty! Good heavens!!" and then, with the air of one who will be scrupulously just, he added: "One of the poor wantons had a certain cadaverous grace." '[1]

It is difficult to refuse Gosse's contemporary testimony quite apart from the conviction that James — a master of the *mot juste* Violet Hunt called him — is likelier to have described a young actress than a fashionable hostess as a 'poor wanton'. It is the more difficult to accept Benson's memory of a thirty-year-old event when we have already discovered reason to suspect him of embroidering his memories. It seems almost certain that the longer and more complicated form which Benson gave to a simple and pithy *mot* arose from his wish to cast it in an unmistakably Jacobean mould; that in fact throughout his whole circumstantial tale he took licence (reasonable or unreasonable) to adorn a balder — and a better — narrative.

Ford Madox Hueffer (Ford Madox Ford) was an even more repetitive and a much less rewarding author of reminiscence. I cannot claim to have determined in how many volumes he told anecdotes of Henry James. Four are listed at the end of this book, a fifth was devoted to memories of Joseph Conrad and a sixth was a critical appraisal of James's writings: there are also several articles in scattered periodicals. The germ of every one of his stories of any interest about James appears in *Thus to Revisit* (1921), itself a re-hash of articles which had come in for a certain amount of criticism when they first appeared in the *English Review*. And not only the germ of the stories: certain images and phrases — the greater writers in England at the turn of the century living each on his particular hill and the lesser writers on their 'little monticules', Ellen Terry waving a gracious hand from her garden above the old tower at Winchelsea — so delighted their coiner that he must repeat them almost *ad nauseam* in his later books. Hueffer, the reader of these books is likely to conclude, was pleased with himself as a writer and perhaps not less as a man. His most

---

[1] In her novel *The Limit* (1911) Ada Leverson quoted James's words, thitherto unpublished, almost verbatim from Gosse. She identified the visitors as the tedious and self-righteous wives of the local doctor and clergyman. Lewis Hind in *Naphtali* (1926), quoting an unnamed witness, substituted 'langourous' for 'cadaverous', while Hueffer (1938) categorized the poor wantons as 'jaded'.

frequent repetitions are of compliments paid to himself by greater men. He told over and over again how Conrad during a collaboration described a phrase of his (Hueffer's) as 'genius'; he was untiringly pleased to think himself the original of Merton Densher — that longish, leanish, fairish, educated, cultivated young English gentleman — in James's *Wings of the Dove*; he continually reminded his readers that James when speaking to Conrad 'always' spoke of himself (Hueffer) as '*votre ami, le jeune homme modeste*'.

Hueffer on occasions openly invented. 'I will begin this work with a little romance in the style of the Master . . .' The 'romance' that begins the essay on James in *Mightier than the Sword* is a brilliant piece of pastiche: Hueffer's imaginative inventions are often more plausible than the conscientious efforts at recollection of more sober historians. Such acknowledged fiction is legitimate — though one may as legitimately wonder why a man who more than once 'after reflection [laid] claim to a very considerable degree of intimacy with James' should need to fall back on invention. Legitimate also, though unacknowledged as fiction, is Hueffer's illustration in the same book of how in his hearing James used to dictate. A favourite remark of James's, another writer tells us, was 'So there, in a manner of speaking, we all were.' Hueffer represents James as working over this with his amanuensis until the sentence has become 'So that here, not so much locally, though to be sure we're here, but at least temperamentally in a manner of speaking, we all are.' For such a purpose of illustration one phrase is no doubt as good as another. But when it comes to reports of speeches not on the face of them invented, any reader with these examples in mind, and with the knowledge of Hueffer's lapse of memory over the appearance of Lamb House (he was by his own account frequently in and out of Lamb House), may be excused if he prefers to suspend belief. Sometimes it comes to inconsistencies so palpable that belief is out of the question. One example is enough to explain why, though Hueffer contributed perhaps a greater volume of anecdotes — excellent stories many of them — to the James legend than any other writer, he is proportionately less quoted than any other writer in this book. The example has been chosen for its brevity: some of Hueffer's recollected conversations with James run into hundreds of words.

In *Thus to Revisit* (and again in *Return to Yesterday* ten years later) Hueffer wrote:

I remember only one occasion on which Henry James spoke of his own work. That was like this: He had published the *Sacred Fount*, and was walking along beside the little shipyard at the foot of Rye Hill. Suddenly he said:

'You understand, . . . I *wanted* to write *The Great Good Place* and *The Altar of the Dead* . . . There are things one wants to write all one's life, but one's artist's conscience prevents one . . . And then . . . perhaps one allows oneself . . .'

I don't know what he meant . . .

Now if we are to believe that there was but the one occasion when James, suddenly and dramatically, spoke of his own work to Hueffer and that that occasion was soon after the publication of *The Sacred Fount* in 1901, what are we to make of a conversation in a third book of Hueffer's in which James is represented as speaking in quite other tones of *The Wings of the Dove* (1902)? And what are we to make of the version of the Master's words, recorded above — now on internal evidence thrown back to 1900 — which Hueffer gives in the third book (*Mightier than the Sword*)? —

Once he stopped suddenly on the road and said, speaking very fast:

'You've read my last volume? . . . There's a story in it . . .' He continued gazing intently at me, then as suddenly he began again: 'There are subjects one thinks of treating all one's life . . . And one says they are not for one. And one says one must not treat them . . . all one's life. All one's life . . . And then suddenly . . . one does . . . *Voilà!*' He had been speaking with almost painful agitation. He added much more calmly: 'One has yielded to temptation. One is to that extent dishonoured. One must make the best of it.'

That story was *The Great Good Place*, appearing, I think, in the volume called *The Soft Side*.

This may be genius, but it is not history.

Many other inconsistencies could be proved against Hueffer. A more serious charge, at present unproven, I shall bring in the hope that it many lead to the production of conclusive evidence, for or against.

Hueffer wrote of James 'hating' Flaubert, a suggestion completely at variance not only with the published evidence but with an entry confided by James after Flaubert's death to a private notebook.[1] He attributed this hatred to 'a deep and never forgotten sense of injury' resulting from two incidents — a snub allegedly administered to James by Flaubert over a point of style in Mérimée, and Flaubert's reception of James and Turgenev in a dressing-gown. Hueffer's account of the incident of the dressing-gown need only be compared with James's own allusion in the preface to *Madame Bovary*, 1902 (reproduced in *Notes on Novelists*), to be seen to be grossly exaggerated. The incident of the snub is more difficult to dispose of. Hueffer gives his source as Flaubert's correspondence. Now there is no allusion to James by name in any one of Flaubert's letters in the comprehensive Conard edition, nor any allusion to any such incident relating to Mérimée; but there is, in a letter from Flaubert to George Sand, an account of a rebuff administered to 'l'Américain H . . .' (identified in the Conard edition and elsewhere as Henry Harrisse) who had spoken slightingly of the writing of Saint-Simon. Richard Aldington in his preface to a selection of Oscar Wilde's works, 1946, tells the story of James as though his identity with 'H . . .' were established; but it is almost, though not absolutely, certain that at the date of the rebuff, which took place in Paris in late June or early July 1874, James was in Baden–Baden. According to his own account James was first introduced to Flaubert by Turgenev, whom he first met in November 1875.

There is another reason for approaching Hueffer's statements with caution. Within a few months of Conrad's death he published *Joseph Conrad, a Personal Remembrance*. That book has been proved to be inaccurate in some details and misleading in others. Hueffer made claims — particularly regarding his help in supplying Conrad with plots for stories — which not only were

[1] For James's affectionate tribute to Flaubert, written soon after the latter's death, see *The Notebooks* (1947), p. 26.

indignantly and somewhat emotionally denied by Mrs Conrad
but which do not tally with documents of Conrad's subsequently
published. What then of his claim to 'a very considerable degree
of intimacy' with James? We have only Hueffer's word for this. In
his letters of the period James was lavish of affectionate phrases
about certain of his friends but he seems seldom to have
mentioned Hueffer, and then only rather casually. Several of
these friends, men of greater intellectual calibre and more modest
bearing than Hueffer, men also whose friendships with James
were more enduring than Hueffer's, have put it on record that real
intimacy of friendship came hard to James; the occasions when he
confided to them any fact about his personal life — apart from
current bulletins about his health — were so rare as to call, in
their writings about him, for special comment. (An example of
this appears under the heading 'The Lamp at the Window' on page
147 below.) Hueffer makes an occasional assertion or innuendo
about James's private life for which I have found no confirmation
elsewhere. We know on James's own authority that before he was
twenty he suffered an injury that placed him *hors de combat* in
the American Civil War and affected him all his life: to that injury
has often been attributed, rightly or wrongly, his failure to
marry. We also know on his own authority that James had a deep
affection for his cousin Minnie Temple (the original of more than
one of his novel heroines) who died of tuberculosis when she was
twenty-four and he was twenty-seven: it is often concluded,
rightly or wrongly, that he was in love with her and but for her
health or his injury might have wished to marry her. It is possible
to speculate — many writers have speculated — on his emo-
tional attitudes, and even his physical disabilities, in later life;
but there is little evidence on which to form an acceptable theory.
The testimony of Hueffer in default of confirmation from a
more reputable source has not seemed worth including in this
book.

It may be as well to interject here a warning against a literal
interpretation of one passage in *Mightier than the Sword*. Much
of the essay on James in that book is misleadingly allusive. James,
says Hueffer, 'had had two great passions — one for a cousin

whom he was to have married and who died of consumption while they were both very young, and the other for a more conspicuous but less satisfactory personage who . . . let him down mercilessly.' There is a certain amount about Minnie Temple ('whom', Hueffer categorically asserts, 'he was to have married') interspersed with an equal amount about 'the other attachment [which] was completely detrimental to him', the 'misfortune that, for a second time, shattered his life'; but there is no overt allusion anywhere in the essay to the theatre, and a reader unaware of Hueffer's theory, expressed in another book, of the embitterment of James's later life by his failure as a playwright might pardonably fail to appreciate that this second and detrimental grand passion was for the Tragic Muse.[1]

As examples of the danger of telling the same tale too often Benson and Hueffer do not stand alone. Two days after James's death in 1916 Violet Hunt ('Mrs Hueffer') contributed to the *Daily Mail* a gossipy but affectionate impression of him. She had known him since her childhood and her article is full of quotable reminiscences. Several of these she later adapted for her book *The Flurried Years* (1926), where hardly one of them appears without some variation from the text of the article; the variations mostly tend towards putting more, or more emphatic, words — a new epithet, a new parenthesis, emphatic capitals or italics — into James's mouth. These enlarged phrases may be authentic and may have fallen victims to the Procrustean methods of Fleet Street: or they may not. In either case it is impossible now to decide what words the Master actually spoke.

A rather different problem is presented by Logan Pearsall Smith. He knew James as intimately as any man who lived to

[1] Lyon N. Richardson in his introduction to *Henry James, Representative Selections* (1941) fell into this trap.

Hueffer maintains that James's new complexity of style, whether in speaking or writing, which he seems to date from about 1900, was a direct psychological reaction to the theatrical débâcle. The theory is scarcely tenable. Hueffer also incidentally detects only two stylistic periods in James's writings, one before and one after 1900. Other critics have detected three — Philip Guedalla's 'simple dynastic arrangement . . . James I, James II and the Old Pretender.'

celebrate the centenary of the Master's birth. The narrative quoted on page 154 from *Unforgotten Years* is no more bald than anything else from this decorative pen, nor is it unconvincing. Yet it would be a poor compliment to a great imagination to take literally the passage on pages 196-7 extracted from his centenary article 'Slices of Cake' in the *New Statesman*, or other vivid passages in that article too long to find a place in this book. This requires no corroborative detail to give it artistic verisimilitude: nor is corroboration possible. It is the only extract here printed, apart from a few with contradictions warningly juxtaposed, of which I cannot conscientiously say that I believe it to contain an appreciable element of literal truth: it is admitted to the canon as spiritually true.

Enough has been said to show that Henry James's chroniclers cannot always be trusted to represent him faithfully. But there are inaccuracies of another kind — errors of dates and places — which suggest some of the pitfalls in the road of the seeker after truth. George Moore retailed in book after book conversations which some of his interlocutors have not scrupled to call imaginary. No one would expect absolute accuracy from his individual and often highly romanticized confessions, memoirs and avowals. Yet one might have looked for something approaching it when he descended from flights of imagination to plain portraiture. In his sketch of James at a conversazione at the Robinsons' (page 26) he speaks of 'the great expanse of closely shaven face' at a date, 1885, when James was full-bearded. The description was written more than thirty years later and during some half of those years Moore was familiar (at a distance, for the friendship of the two men had lapsed) with a clean-shaven James. His memory played him false: and if it did so in this particular, how much more probable that it should have done so when he came to record as though verbatim, after more than thirty years, the conversation on Pater and Christianity printed on page 102.

The next example comes from 'Henry James's High Hat', a chapter in Hugh Walpole's book of reminiscences *The Apple Trees*. It concerns one of the most poignant episodes in James's career, the failure of his play *Guy Domville* in 1895; it concerns a

visit by James and Walpole to an Oscar Wilde revival at an
uncertain date not long before the 1914 war; and it was published
in 1932. James, Walpole says,

took me with him that he might see for the first time *The Importance of
Being Earnest*. This was the play that had been filling the Haymarket at
the very moment when *Guy Domville* had been failing so dismally at the
St James's, and he had described to me before how, when *Domville* had
been running for a week or so, he went one evening to the theatre to find
it half empty, and then had walked across the Square to see 'House Full'
boards outside the Haymarket. He had refused to see Wilde's play until
this long-after revival. He saw it, found it miserable trash . . .

Now this account is riddled with inaccuracies. *The Importance
of Being Earnest* was *not* on at the Haymarket during the brief run
(5 January to 5 February 1895) of *Guy Domville*, though *An Ideal
Husband* was: *The Importance of Being Earnest* was first
produced at the St James's, where it followed Henry James's play
on 14 February. James did *not* go to the St James's when *Domville*
had been running for a week or so and find the theatre half
empty: between the second night (7 January) when he told two
correspondents there was a good house[1] and almost the last night
of the run a month later we have his contemporary word for it
that he did not go near the theatre.[2] The memorable occasion on
which by his own account he 'walked across the Square' was his
own first night, and he did *not* walk from the St James's to the
Haymarket but from the Haymarket, where he had sat through
An Ideal Husband, to the St James's.[3]

Here we have not so much a conflict of evidence — for the
records of 1895 are unassailable — as grounds for inquiry into the
origin of a myth. Had Henry James forgotten by 1913 (Wilde's
Earnest was revived in 1909, 1911 and 1913) what had happened
on one of the blackest of his life's black-letter days in 1895? And
did he in fact tell Walpole what Walpole says he told him? Or did

[1] This is confirmed by contemporary press comment.
[2] The letter is dated 2 February; the last performance was on 5 February.
[3] Quoted below, page 88.

Walpole in 1932 misremember[1] what James had said some twenty years earlier? It does not much matter, for the inaccuracy is proved. But it makes one wonder what other seemingly well-attested incidents in the *Domville* myth where proof is impossible may not be fabrications.

The failure of *Guy Domville* and of James's theatrical ambitions generally has given rise to many strange statements but to none more strange than this, from a passage on novelists-turned-playwrights in the memoirs of Geneviève Ward: 'Poor James . . . used to sit in torture behind the curtains of his box, registering every hiss on his heart strings, and when it was over finding no relief but tears as he rushed from the house, while gallery and pit, with their thumbs down, were roaring "Author! Author!" for the final sacrifice.'

'Used to sit . . .' Of the four of James's plays produced in his life-time one only was not courteously received on its first performance — *Guy Domville*. Hissing was something so unusual in the West End theatre of that period that the *Graphic* hung a disquisition on the 'ethics' of it on the peg of — *Guy Domville*. Yet can Miss Ward with her suggestion of several occasions have intended even the sole occasion of the first night of *Guy Domville*? On that night James did not sit in torture in a box: he entered the theatre by the stage door as the curtain fell on the last act. The whole story is told on pages 86–94 of this book and further comment would be superfluous. One cannot but wish that Miss Ward had exchanged this flight of fancy in her memoirs for even a footnote on the play — *Tenants* — which James wrote for her in 1890 but in which she never appeared.

If the most that can be charged against Moore and Walpole is a faulty memory and against Geneviève Ward an exuberant

---

[1] Walpole's memory was at fault when he wrote in the same chapter of H. G. Wells having compared James (in his 'third manner') to an 'elephant picking up a pea'. Wells's words in *Boon* were: 'leviathan retrieving pebbles . . . a magnificent but painful hippopotamus resolved at any cost, even at the cost of its dignity, upon picking up a pea which has got into a corner of its den.' There are also inconsistencies between Walpole's *Apple Trees* (1932) and his article on James in *Horizon*, (1940).

credulity, with the next example of proved inaccuracy it is less easy to acquit the narrator of some malice. It is from the *Life* of Thomas Hardy, ostensibly written by his widow but now known to have been written by Hardy himself:

It should be explained that this Rabelais Club, which had a successful existence for many years, had been instituted by Sir Walter Besant . . . as a declaration for virility in literature. Hardy was pressed to join as being the most virile writer of works of imagination then in London: while, it may be added, Henry James after a discussion was rejected for the lack of that quality, though he was afterwards invited as a guest.

This, about James, is gratuitous: it is also wholly untrue — as Hardy might have discovered for himself with little trouble. His own copies of the *Recreations* of the Rabelais Club lie before me as I write: in each of the three volumes (which were still in Mrs Hardy's possession when she brought out 'her' book) James's name appears in the list of members, in the first with the asterisk that distinguishes a foundation member. The club was a strange product of late Victorianism. Virility ('in literature') is not easy to define; Rabelaisianism perhaps little more so. Besant, besides being a vigorous sub-Dickensian novelist, was the author of a book about Rabelais. But in what were old Sir Frederick Pollock and his sons Rabelaisian? or Comyns Carr of the Grosvenor Gallery? Among later members Henley was once described by James as 'rude, boisterous, windy, headstrong' — all no doubt Rabelaisian qualities; but what of Meredith and Egerton Castle? Some of Hardy's novels, to his generation, were shocking in their treatment of sex, but that is hardly the same thing. And what of Henry James himself? Not virile — 'in literature'? not Rabelaisian? One of the best contemporary criticisms of James's 'third manner' — best because unsparing yet inoffensive as only criticism from a close and trusted friend can be — is to be found in a letter which his brother William wrote to him when *The American Scene* was published. The passage begins briefly with praise of the book; goes on at length to deplore on well-argued grounds the 'manner' (a manner which William himself at times when writing of it almost contagiously echoes); and pertinently to our present purpose concludes:

Well, the verve and animal spirits with which you can keep your method going, first on one place then on another, through all those tightly printed pages is something marvellous; and there are pages surely doomed to be immortal, those on the 'drummers', *e.g.*, at the beginning of 'Florida'. They are in the best sense Rabelaisian.

Hardy had little love for Henry James. After James's death there appeared the *Letters*, and in them an often quoted passage which may best be reproduced here with Hardy's introductory sarcasm and interpolated question-mark:

Hardy's good-natured friends Henry James and R. L. Stevenson (whom he afterwards called the Polonius and the Osric of novelists) corresponded about it in this vein: 'Oh, yes, dear Louis: *Tess of the d'Urbervilles* is vile. The pretence of sexuality is only equalled by the absence of it [?], and the abomination of the language by the author's reputation for style.'

Hardy lived to see James's comment printed. It is easy to understand that he may have been angered. The suspicion that he wished to retaliate upon James by emphasizing his seeming disloyalty is strengthened by the failure to quote James's tribute to *Tess* — also in a letter to Stevenson — as having in spite of its faults 'a singular beauty and charm'.

The point is of importance here only in so far that any known prejudice or animosity must be taken into account in assessing the reliability of witnesses to the James legend. A word must be said about one widespread prejudice in particular.

There was a time — now long past — when a number of James's compatriots resented his decision to leave America, to extol the Old World at the expense of the New, to represent in his novels (as it seemed to some) that Americans unless they lived abroad were lacking in the finer perceptions, to misrepresent (as it seemed to others) American girlhood. Among many quips Colonel Higginson in the 'eighties replied to someone who had said that James was a cosmopolitan, 'Hardly, for a cosmopolitan is at home even in his own country.' America wished to read him, or even to know about him, so little that at a public function in the 'nineties an allusion to 'the late Henry James' is said to have passed without protest. It was not that he failed of appreciation

among the discriminating: when a second batch of seven acade-
micians was elected to the American Academy of Letters and Arts
in 1905 Henry James and Henry Adams alone were elected unani-
mously. But the prejudice at a lower level smouldered on: it
flared up with his naturalization as a British subject when Britain,
but not yet America, was involved in war.

A good example of this prejudice, outside the normal run of
ill-natured gossip, may be found in the 'Personal Recollections of
Henry James' contributed by E. S. Nadal to *Scribner's Magazine*
in 1920. Nadal had known James off and on since the 'seventies
when both were living in London. He is preoccupied almost
throughout his article with James's attitude towards America and
Americans, and he ends it with a regretful picture of the American James that might have been. (Perhaps he had not read 'The
Jolly Corner'.) He gives the impression of a man endeavouring to
do justice in the face of odds to the memory of an old friend. The
odds are James's anglophilia; and the acidulous tone into which
Nadal is sometimes betrayed does not do justice to his
endeavour. That at least one of the anecdotes as related is impossible and another scarcely credible matters less in this context
than that in the aggregate they leave an impression very different
from what the writer appears to have intended. To this extent
Nadal cannot be held to be a satisfactory witness.

The American prejudice of which I have spoken finally died
with the great revival of interest in James's technical achievement in the 1930s. In that revival American scholars and critics
took the lead; the Master has been restored to eminence in the
native hierarchy. But while it lasted the prejudice did his reputation incalculable harm. It encouraged the telling of unflattering
anecdotes, as often based on malice as on fact and as often told
by those who had never, as by those who had scarcely, known
him. Many such stories appeared in American gossip columns
and American books of reminiscence, particularly during the ten
years immediately after James's death. Many of them are known
on this side of the Atlantic only at second or third telling or from
vague allusions now difficult — even were it worth while — to
follow up. In a biography in 1924 of Stephen Crane, another

American novelist who lived for some time in England though he died a loyal American citizen, Thomas Beer painted a portrait of Henry James which but for the mention of his name must have seemed unrecognizable to the reader of, say, Arthur Benson or Gosse or Edith Wharton. To Beer, though not to Crane (a circumstance which makes the inclusion of the portrait in the biography seem gratuitous), no word is too harsh for James. His motives were mercenary, his egotism astonishing, his literary criticism consummately silly; he was 'a coloured and complicated ritual', 'the pet of cynical voluptuaries', 'a provincial sentimentalist touted by worshippers as the last flower of European culture'. This is of course a point of view. But as the artist seems rigidly to have selected for his portrait only those pieces of second-hand gossip that tend to belittle James's more, and to magnify his less, amiable features one must conclude that it is the point of view of a caricaturist.

It is arguable that the portrait of James painted by his 'worshippers' — and he did not lack uncritical admirers — is no less of a caricature. Certainly the 'worship' contributed to the legend, though not so much directly as because its exaggerations were obvious and fair game for those who were set upon ridiculing the object worshipped. The credibility as witnesses to James's character of those who admired him most must be tested as thoroughly as that of those who admired him not at all; but clearly a writer who, having known him, concentrated upon the good in him is more likely to add to the sum of truth than one who, not having known him, writes only ill of him. For this reason I have quoted more freely from Mrs Humphry Ward than from Mr Thomas Beer. Mrs Ward's admiration was extreme: so much is clear from her reminiscences whether or not we accept Beer's second-hand story that she 'fell speechless and scarlet' when someone said that one of James's stories was derived from one of Maupassant's.[1] But even if it was extreme, and although the expressions of affection with which she and other women of

---

[1] James openly acknowledged that his story 'Paste' arose out of 'the ingenious thought of transposing the terms of one of Guy de Maupassant's admirable *contes* . . . *La Parure*'.

her generation wrote of James after his death are saccharine to the modern palate, the fact that he inspired affection is an essential fact. James in one aspect was a figure of fun — to those who did not know him, to those that scarcely knew him, to his friends, even at times to himself; in another of his aspects he was, to contemporary and younger writers, 'the Master'; in yet another he was the object of — call it 'worship' if you will: the word in vogue at the time was 'love'. It is not irrelevant that he drew to himself the affection of uncritical women (though in other relations certainly Mrs Ward was not uncritical) as well as of his intellectual equals among men.

I have dealt so far mainly with negative considerations — evidence of what James was not or of what he did not do or did not say — and with false or hostile witnesses. For a positive portrait, for what he was, the reader must turn from this introduction to the extracts that compose the book and must form his own opinion. The extracts are drawn from hostile as well as friendly witnesses — nothing is extenuated though somewhat is set down that others wrote in malice — but a word about the credibility of the friendly witnesses may not be out of place.

The best are those (such as Arthur Benson, Edmund Gosse and Miss Bosanquet) who knew James well but whose affection stopped short of idolatry; those whose most characteristic stories are as often against themselves as against him (Edith Wharton, Desmond MacCarthy, Hugh Walpole); and those few who, confronted only rarely by this dominating but ambiguous personality, remained impartial (such as Arnold Bennett). The first group may be left to speak for themselves. Of Mrs Wharton, in the second group, a recent writer has described as 'overwritten' her portrait of a 'helpless, complicated, timorous great man': but if Mrs Wharton and others saw James so at times, she drew him also as an anything but helpless or timorous critic, to her own face, of her own fiction (pages 136–8). Walpole and MacCarthy could both, by the extraction of phrases out of context, be represented as hostile, though their appreciation of James's more admirable traits is likely to remain longer with the reader of their essays on him. More significant perhaps is James as a teller of stories against himself. I have said that he saw himself at times as a figure of fun. There is abundant evidence of this in the extracts. He knew that in conversation he 'mountained mole-hills'; that his gesticulations — in which the touch of humour was half-conscious — could lead him into social disaster; that in his absent-mindedness he was capable of not recognizing his own cook; that he must appear ignorant and unathletic to children; and that his figure was indeed unathletic. The attentive reader of the extracts may suspect that if at times he posed, at other times he posed as posing, and that those for whom his little performances were staged might have been less glib to recount them if they had realized how much their own ingenuousness contributed to the comedy. A characteristic in late life of which he was well aware was what has been called his 'innocent malice'. But malice however innocent in intention is seldom innocuous in effect, and some of the comments he made about his friends — Hardy, Mrs Ward, Mrs Wharton — behind their backs have been grist to the mills of his detractors. Again the reader must judge for himself; but the point will illustrate the conclusion that in the character of James, as perhaps of most men, each of two contradictory estimates may be true.

E. V. Lucas met James only once — in about 1913 — and was shocked by the malicious tone of his comments upon people: it was at the Sidney Colvins' where the atmosphere, at once 'literary' and intimate, may have seemed to James as propitious to innocent malice, and as safe, as were the houses of Edith Wharton and Howard Sturgis. At much the same period Reginald Blomfield and A. G. Bradley, men as eminent and as discriminating in their own fields as Colvin and Lucas in theirs, formed of James in the very different society of Rye the opinion that he was forbearing of criticism, kind-hearted and sympathetic, full of consideration for others, modest and even diffident. Who will confidently say that Lucas was right and Blomfield wrong, or Blomfield right and Lucas wrong? There is truth in both impressions, though that truth may reveal at least as much about Lucas and Blomfield as about James. It is the same when we attempt to answer the question from which we started — had James, as Hardy maintained, a ponderously warm manner of saying nothing in infinite sentences, or did he always, as Anstey held, reach at the last a point well worth waiting for? Hugh Walpole was sometimes bored to pins and needles by a manner of conversation which Arthur Benson regarded as by far the richest species of intellectual performance he had ever been privileged to hear. From this we learn that James appeared as different things to different men. He bored Hardy and Walpole, he did not bore Anstey and Benson; he shocked Lucas and charmed Blomfield — and was 'worshipped', it may be (though we have not her word for it), by Mrs Humphry Ward. Perhaps these varied impressions belong rather to estimates of the characters of those who received them than to a book of extracts about the man who created them.

There remains one other class of witness — the silent witness. Many of his friends — Lady Prothero, Mrs Clifford, Howard Sturgis, above all his distinguished literary friends in France — seem not to have written about James at all. Others wrote indeed but nothing greatly to the point. Among those that did write, formally or in correspondence, there are some who failed to tell us just what we might wish to know. It is tantalizing that Howells, passing through London in 1897, should have spent two days 'continuously and exclusively' with James, should never have seen him 'more divinely interesting', but should have failed to tell his correspondent what they discussed. Dame Ethel Smyth's most vivid recollection by far of 'the only real blazing theatre triumph' she ever had — at Covent Garden in 1902 — was of James's compliment to her curtsey at the Royal Box: it is tantalizing that modesty should have deterred her from recording it. Perhaps most tantalizing of all is to be told by Mrs Comyns Carr that her own and other children at a house-party were entertained with a game of 'Definitions' by — of all the literary figures of the age — Meredith and James, and not to be told what they defined or how they defined it.

*   *   *

So much for 'the Legend', but what of the 'Master'?[1] I am

---

[1] The honorific seems to have been bestowed on James early in the 'nineties. Gertrude Atherton who was assiduous at the social and literary salons of London during the 1895 season writes: 'Henry James, and deservedly, was spoken of with bated breath as "the Master".'

conscious of some temerity in placing upon my title-page a sobriquet which others have used of James partly or wholly in derision. Hueffer used it habitually in his books; the Ranee of Sarawak who by her own account was 'not literary' commonly addressed James to his face as 'dear Master'; H. G. Wells says that James 'plainly' — one wonders how he made it plain — regretted that '*Cher Maître*' was not an English expression. Nor is it perhaps enough that Conrad, writing letters to James or presenting his own books to him, used the French phrase. Nor again is it entirely that James entitled the best known of his short stories about men of letters (it was in no sense a self-portrait) 'The Lesson of the Master'.

This book of extracts deals not at all with James's literary achievement; and only with his literary fame during his life in so far as there would have been no legend of James the man if he had not achieved fame as a writer. The lasting quality of that fame was questioned when after his death he fell into the trough of the wave of reputation. The generation of Gerard Hopkins successively 'gloried in James, suffered from James and escaped from James'. But in time James rose from his trough, as Tennyson and Trollope and other submerged Victorians have risen from theirs, and he is now on the crest of a new wave. The new reputation is different from that, or those, of his prime. There is now no bearded young cosmopolitan author of *Daisy Miller* to be fêted in London drawing-rooms and fought shy of in New York; no chronicler in three-volume fiction of Paris and London stage life to be taken up — and dropped — by actor-managers; no writer of tales of authors to become a feather in the cap of the *Yellow Book*; nor yet an Old Pretender whose 'difficult' novels every young pretender to intellect must at least claim to have read and enjoyed and understood. These reputations were real enough, even if at their height 'I don't sell ten copies'. The new reputation is of a more, a wholly, impersonal kind. A new generation — whether more or less sophisticated than Hopkins's is difficult to say — besieged the second-hand booksellers of London during the Second World War clamouring for James's novels, long out of print. A new generation of critics, impersonal as surgeons (or as the psychoanalysts from whom many of them borrow their terminology), has examined the body of his work, cut it open, laid bare the entrails, dissected, analysed, reassembled and restored — if not 'the', at least 'a' Master: a Master both in his own right and as a major influence upon the novel-writing of the twentieth century.

In this book I have attempted to show James the man as others saw him, and as far as possible in those others' words. His own writings are not relevant except in so far as a letter or telegram may suggest what the recipient thought of the sender. The justification of such a collection of extracts can only be that it should send new readers to his novels, reminiscences and letters, and for this reason the novels and reminiscences are not quoted at all and the formal collection of *Letters*, edited by Percy Lubbock, has been used, apart from the chapter headed 'Theatricals', only for an occasional elucidatory footnote.

Most of the chapters are arranged by subject as the material does not lend itself readily to chronological treatment. The chapter on the theatre however is on a strictly chronological plan, and for this purpose it would have been unreasonable not to use some of the letters which Mr Lubbock had carefully selected. The different plan and scale of this chapter were chosen partly because James's 'dramatic lustrum' is the best documented period as well as one of the most interesting periods of his life, and partly because much of the documentation dates from after Leon Edel published in Paris in 1931 his *Henry James, Les années dramatiques*.

In order to distinguish them from incidents recollected in tranquillity or emotion, extracts from documents contemporary with the events recorded have been dated at the foot or in a footnote. With E. F. Benson's warning, and example, about depending upon documents I should perhaps say that I have departed from the text of the authors quoted only in attempting some sort of uniformity of spelling, capital letters, stops, quotation marks and italics. Omissions (save in two much abbreviated passages from Violet Hunt) and corrections of all but the most obvious errors are clearly indicated.

(1946)

THE MASTER

PARTIAL PORTRAITS

London c. 1878

I remember Henry James when he was really Henry James jun., come to London and fêted everywhere on the strength of a little story in the *Corhill*.[1] He was tall, rather thick-set, with an olive skin. 'Mamma,' I said, 'he looks as if he ought to be wearing earrings.' This was the impression made on a child by this Elizabethan, with his dark, silky beard and deep, wonderful eyes.

Violet Hunt

London 1882

Stretched on a sofa and apologizing for not rising to greet me, his appearance gave me a little shock, for I had not thought of him as an invalid. He hurriedly and rather evasively declared that he was not that, but that a muscular weakness of his spine obliged him, as he said, 'to assume the horizontal posture' during some hours of every day in order to bear the almost unbroken routine of evening engagements . . . I recall his appearance, seen then for the first time by daylight; there was something shadowy about it, the face framed in dark brown hair cut short in the Paris fashion, and an equally dark beard, rather loose and 'fluffy'. He was in deep mourning, his mother having died five or six months earlier . . . His manner was grave, extremely courteous, but a little formal and frightened, which seemed strange in a man living in constant communication with the world.

Edmund Gosse

[1] 'Daisy Miller', published in the *Cornhill Magazine* in June-July 1878.

London 1885

A flutter of feminine attention began at once about the important American, and while he talked in his pompous but not unfriendly manner, addressing his conversation by turns to Mary and Mabel Robinson, a little careless, I thought, of the attentions of Vernon Lee and her admirations of his style, I was left to my meditations, and these began in a recollection of Henry James's size, which seemed to have enlarged since I last saw him — a man of great bulk and such remoteness that one did not associate him with *The Portrait of a Lady*. He did not carry my thoughts towards a man who had known women at first hand and intimately, but one who had watched them with literary rather than personal interest. And these thoughts drew my eyes to the round head, already going bald, to the small dark eyes closely set, and to the great expanse of closely shaven face.[1] His legs were short, and his hands and feet large; and he sat portentously in his chair, speaking with some hesitation and great care, anxious that every sentence, or if not all, at least every third of fourth, should send forth a beam of humour.

George Moore

Worcestershire 1885

It was at Broadway that Sargent made a full-face drawing of Henry James. The drawing, which pleased no one, was a complete failure and was destroyed, Sargent saying it was 'impossible to do justice to a face that was all covered with beard like a bear'. The following year he did a fine profile, reproduced first in the *Yellow Book*.

Evan Charteris

[1] James was full-bearded at this date.

Paris c. 1888

Henry James often came to Paris, where he had numerous friends
. . . He took a great fancy to Frazier and often wandered into the
studio in the rue Madame. He was charming to all of us; he liked
young people, and all his life he had been closely associated with
painters and sculptors. I was amused by his slow and exact way
of speaking. He was not in those days so massive as he became
later, either in person or manner, but was already elaborately
precise and correct. He always carried his silk hat, stick and
gloves into the room when paying a call, laying hat and gloves
across his knee.

William Rothenstein

London c. 1890

He was always well-dressed; perhaps even a little more than that,
for he gave the impression — with his rather conspicuous spats
and extra shiny boots — of having just come from an ultra-smart
wedding ceremony.

C. C. H. Millar

Rome 1894

I've only caught sight of James again in carriages with people in
swell clothes and footmen. I think the man James is just a little
of a snob, with all his pretensions of hating people, and he evidently thought he had a suit of duds just like the middle-class
Italian — of ten years ago, it's true; but to-day that person is a
combination of the Frenchman of 1830 and an Englishman of last
year — and H. J. don't look like that.

Joseph Pennell, 1894

London 1895

In the 'nineties he was in appearance almost remarkably unremarkable; his face might have been anybody's face; it was as though, when looking round for a face, he had been able to find nothing to his taste and had been obliged to put up with a ready-made 'stock' article until something more suitable could be made to order expressly for him. This special and only genuine Henry James's face was not 'delivered' until he was a comparatively old man, so that for the greater part of his life he went about in disguise. My mother, who was devoted to his works, used to be especially annoyed by this elusive personality. 'I always want so much to talk with him,' she complained, 'yet when I meet him I never can remember who he is.'

W. Graham Robertson

After 1900

I have said that in early life Henry James was not 'impressive'; as time went on his appearance became, on the contrary, excessively noticeable and arresting. He removed the beard which had long disguised his face, and so revealed the strong lines of mouth and chin, which responded to the majesty of the skull. In the breadth and smoothness of the head — Henry James became almost wholly bald early in life — there was at length something sacerdotal. As time went on he grew less and less Anglo-Saxon in appearance and more Latin. I remember once seeing a canon preaching in the Cathedral of Toulouse who was the picture of Henry James in his unction, his gravity and his vehemence. Sometimes there could be noted — what Henry would have hated to think existing — a theatrical look which struck the eye, as though he might be some retired *jeune premier* of the Français, *jeune* no longer; and often the prelatical expression faded into a fleeting likeness to one or other celebrated Frenchman of letters (never to any Englishman or American), somewhat of Lacordaire in the intolerable scrutiny of the eyes, somewhat of Sainte-Beuve, too, in all except the mouth, which though mobile and elastic gave the impression in rest of being small. All these comparisons and suggestions, however, must be taken as the barest hints, intended to mark the tendency of Henry James's radically powerful and unique outer appearance. The beautiful modelling of the brows, waxing and waning under the stress of excitement, is a point which singularly dwells in the memory.

Edmund Gosse

New Forest 1901

I went in the summer to spend a week-end with the Godkins in the New Forest. We arrived in the afternoon. We entered the hall-way and a figure of vaudeville advanced; tight check trousers, waistcoat of a violent pattern, coat with short tails like a cock sparrow — none matching; cravat in a magnificent flowery bow.

Henry Dwight Sedgwick

Winchelsea c. 1902

Oh, Mamma dear! isn't he an elegant fowl!

Borys Conrad, aged about 4

London 1903

In appearance he was not in the least literary. That had been almost a shock to me. One of my earliest impressions of him had been gained from a photograph shewing him resting his head on his hand and looking as if he had written all the literature in the world. I found him a rather over-plump man in his sixties, quite bald and round of face, who would have been classified by an intelligent person who did not know him as a successful lawyer or banker of the old school. It was not until that first dinner was half over, and he suddenly turned and looked at me very closely, that I realized the strange power of Henry James's eyes. They made me

feel in those instants as if he had read me to the soul — and I
rather think he had.

Elizabeth Jordan

New York 1905

Finally he came, dignified and impressive, with manners almost
courtly and wearing a top hat several sizes too big . . . On his
way out Mr James stopped before [a painting] and looked at it a
long time, bending forward, in his top hat, his stick behind him.
'Just one more, please — I must do this, for you look like a
Daumier!' He seemed really amused but remained in the same
position until I photographed him again. Then we shook hands
and he departed. My assistant who had none too much reverence
in her make-up, looking out of the window after he had gone,
said 'He's trying to find the subway and he does look like the Mad
Hatter.'

Alice Boughton[1]

London 1907

We sat in armchairs on either side of a fireless grate while we
observed each other. I suppose he found me harmless and I know
that I found him amazing. He was much more massive than I had
expected, much broader and stouter and stronger. I remembered
that someone had told me he used to be taken for a sea-captain
when he wore a beard, but it was clear that now, with the beard
shaved away, he would hardly have passed for, say, an admiral,
in spite of the keen grey eyes set in a face burned to a colourable
sea-faring brown by the Italian sun. No successful naval officer
could have afforded to keep that sensitive mobile mouth. After
the interview I wondered what kind of impression one might
have gained from a chance encounter in some such observation

[1] Three of Alice Boughton's photographs of James are reproduced in the Henry
James number of *Hound and Horn*, April–May 1934. The 'Daumier' photograph
is there dated in error 1906.

cell as a railway carriage. Would it have been possible to fit him confidently unto any single category? He had reacted with so much success against both the American accent and the English manner that he seemed only doubtfully Anglo-Saxon. He might perhaps have been an eminent cardinal in mufti, or even a Roman senator amusing himself by playing the part of a Sussex squire. The observer could at least have guessed that any part he chose to assume would be finely conceived and generously played, for his features were all cast in the classical mould of greatness. He might very well have been a merciful Caesar or a benevolent Napoleon, and a painter who worked at his portrait a year or two later was excusably reminded of so many illustrious makers of history that he declared it to be a hard task to isolate the individual character of the model.

Theodora Bosanquet

France 1907–1908

The Henry James of the early meetings was the bearded Penseroso of Sargent's delicate drawing, soberly fastidious in dress and manner, cut on the approved pattern of the *homme du monde* of the 'eighties; whereas by the time we got to know each other well the compact upright figure had expanded to a rolling and voluminous outline, and the elegance of dress given way to the dictates of comfort, while a clean shave had revealed in all its sculptural beauty the noble Roman mask and the big dramatic mouth . . .

Though he now affected to humour the lumbering frame whose physical ease must be considered first, he remained spas-modically fastidious about his dress, and about other trifling social observances, and once when he was motoring with us in France in 1907, and suddenly made up his mind (at Poitiers of all places!) that he must then and there buy a new hat, almost insuperable difficulties attended its selection. It was not until he had announced his despair of ever making the hatter understand that 'what he wanted was a hat like everybody else's', and I had rather impatiently suggested his asking for a head-covering '*pour l'homme moyen sensuel'*, that the joke broke through his indecisions, and to a rich accompaniment of chuckles the hat was bought.

Still more particular about his figure than his dress, he resented any suggestion that his silhouette had lost firmness and acquired volume; and once, when my friend Jacques-Emile Blanche was doing the fine seated profile portrait which is the only one that renders him *as he really was*, he privately implored me to suggest to Blanche 'not to lay such stress on the resemblance to Daniel Lambert'.

Edith Wharton

The Eyes

When I look back it seems to me that Henry James was the most profoundly sad-looking man I have ever seen, not even excepting certain members of the house of Rothschild. His eyes were not only age-old and world-weary, as are those of cultured Jews, but they had vision — and one did not like to think of what they saw.

Ella Hepworth Dixon

His eyes were singularly penetrating, dark and a little prominent . . . My servants used to say: 'It always gives me a turn to open the door for Mr James. His eyes seems to look you through to the very backbone.'

F. M. Hueffer

The Smile

No man of letters, I suppose, ever had a more disarming smile than his . . . It was worth losing a train (and sometimes you had to do that) while he rummaged for the right word. During the search the smile was playing about his face, a smile with which he was on such good terms that it was a part of him chuckling at the other parts of him. I remember once meeting him in the street and

asking him how he liked a lecture we had both lately attended. I
did not specially want to know nor he to tell, and as he sought for
the right words it began to rain, and by and by it was raining
heavily. In this predicament he signed to a passing growler and
we got in and it remained there stationary until he reached the
triumphant conclusion, which was that no one could have delivered a lecture with less offence. They certainly were absolutely
the right words, but the smile's enjoyment while he searched for
them was what I was watching. It brought one down like Leather-
stocking's Killdeer.

J. M. Barrie

TALK

GENERAL APPRECIATIONS

[Henry James] has a ponderously warm manner of saying nothing in infinite sentences.

Thomas Hardy, 1886

If ever there was a man that talked like a book — and one of his own books too — that man is Mr Henry James. With grave aspect and in a darkling undertone he pronounces his solemn gnomes and mysterious epigrams, or propounds those social and psychical conundrums which supply his devout admirers the largest part of their intellectual exercise. But as Sir George Trevelyan judiciously observes —

> The gravest of us now and then unbends,
> And likes his glass of claret and his friends.

And when this softening change has passed over Mr James he becomes a delightful companion. He has the desirable qualities of fine appreciation and genuine sympathy; he observes closely and remarks justly; talks, not much indeed but always with tact and discrimination; is always ready to please and be pleased; and, without being in the slightest degree a flatterer or a parasite, enjoys the happy knack of putting those to whom he speaks in good conceit with themselves.

G. W. E. Russell, 1889

In conversation he was meticulously (no other adverb is so appropriate) careful to convey his precise meaning, so that his remarks became a sort of Chinese nest of parentheses; it took him some time to arrive at his point but he always reached it, and it was always well worth waiting for.

F. Anstey

The greatest compliment that can be paid to that subtle, complex mind of his is that, notwithstanding his mannerisms and hesitations that would be so tediously unbearable in the case of most of us, Henry James never came even near to being a bore. One had to wait a long time for the thought to be expressed; one watched the process of its germination and development; but when it came one felt that it had been tremendously worth waiting for, and that it was a thought peculiarly his own and expressed as no other man could have expressed it.

Alfred Sutro

A great deal has been told and written of Henry James's circum-ambulatory speech, of his long and vermicular sentences, his 'ers' and 'ahs', and I had had one experience of it myself. But there were times when he could be as clear and direct and coherent as Edmund Gosse or any other noted conversationalist, and to-day was one of them. In fact he talked as if every sentence had been carefully rehearsed; every semi-colon, every comma, was in exactly the right place, and his rounded periods dropped to the floor and bounced about like tiny rubber balls.

Gertrude Atherton

I loved him, was frightened of him, was bored by him, was staggered by his wisdom and stupefied by his intricacies . . . I was sometimes so bored that I had pins and needles in my legs and arms . . .

His elaborate, intricate sentences, so often imitated (never quite successfully), came from his sense that words were not enough for the things of the mind. That was why, after an infinity of elaboration, the thing that he wanted to say would sometimes emerge at last trivial and unimportant — as though in despair he had let his treasure go because he could not haul it up far enough into the light, and so at last he caught at anything as a substitute.

Hugh Walpole

Impassioned Soliloquy

The extreme and almost tantalizing charm of his talk lay not only in his quick transitions, his exquisite touches of humour and irony, the width and force of his sympathy, the range of his intelligence, but in the fact that the whole process of his thought, the qualifications, the resumptions, the interlineations, were laid bare. The beautiful sentences, so finished, so deliberate, shaped themselves audibly upon the air. It was like being present at the actual construction of a little palace of thought, of improvised yet perfect design. The manner was not difficult to imitate: the slow accumulation of detail, the widening sweep, the interjection of grotesque and emphatic images, the studied exaggerations; but what could not be copied was the firmness of the whole conception. He never strayed loosely, as most voluble talkers do, from subject to subject. The *motif* was precisely enunciated, revised, elongated, improved upon, enriched, but it was always, so to speak, strictly contrapuntal. He dealt with the case and nothing but the case; he completed it, dissected it, rounded it off. It was done with much deliberation and even with both repetition and hesitation. But it was not only irresistibly beautiful, it was by far the richest species of intellectual performance that I have ever been privileged to hear. I must frankly confess that, while I regard the later books with a reverent admiration for their superb fineness and the concentrated wealth of expression, they are hard work, they require unflagging patience and continuous freshness of apprehension. But his talk had none of this weighted quality. It was not exactly conversation; it was more an impassioned soliloquy; but his tone, his gestures, his sympathetic alertness made instantly and abundantly clear and sparkling what on a printed page often became, at least to me, tough and coagulated. There was certainly something pontifical about it — not that it was ever solemn or mysterious; but you had the feeling that it was the natural expansiveness of a great mind and a deep emotion, even when his talk played, as it often did, half lambently and half incisively, over the characters and temperaments of friends and acquaintances. It was minute, but never trivial; and there was tremendous force in the background. Like the steam-hammer, it could smite and bang an incandescent mass, but it could also crack a walnut or pat an egg. It was perfectly adjusted, delicately controlled.

A. C. Benson

Malice and Merriment

His slow way of speech, sometimes mistaken for affectation — or, more quaintly, for an artless form of Aglomania! — was really the partial victory over a stammer which in his boyhood had been thought incurable. The elaborate politeness and the involved phraseology that made off-hand intercourse with him so difficult to casual acquaintances probably sprang from the same defect. To have too much time in which to weigh each word before uttering it could not but lead, in the case of the alertest and most sensitive of minds, to self-consciousness and self-criticism; and this fact explains the hesitating manner that often passed for a mannerism . . .

To James's intimates, however, these elaborate hesitations, far from being an obstacle, were like a cobweb bridge flung from his mind to theirs, an invisible passage over which one knew that silver-footed ironies, veiled jokes, tiptoe malices, were stealing to explode a huge laugh at one's feet. This moment of suspense, in which there was time to watch the forces of malice and merriment assembling over the mobile landscape of his face, was perhaps the rarest of all in the unique experience of a talk with Henry James.

His letters, delightful as they are, give but hints and fragments of his talk; the talk that to his closest friends, when his health and

the surrounding conditions were favourable, poured out in a
series of images so vivid and appreciations so penetrating, the
whole so sunned over by irony, sympathy and wide-flashing fun,
that those who heard him at his best will probably agree in saying
of him what he once said to me of M. Paul Bourget: 'He was the
first, easily, of all the talkers I ever encountered.'

Edith Wharton

Mountaining Mole-hills

In conversation he could not help giving his best, the stereotyped
and perfunctory being abhorrent to him. Each talk was thus a
fresh adventure, an opportunity of discovering for himself what
he thought about books and human beings. His respect for his
subject was only equalled, one noticed, by his respect for that
delicate instrument for recording and comparing impressions, his
own mind. He absolutely refused to hustle it, and his conversational manner was largely composed of reassuring and soothing
gestures intended to allay, or anticipate, signs of impatience. The
sensation of his hand on my shoulder in our pausing rambles
together was, I felt, precisely an exhortation to patience. 'Wait,'
that reassuring pressure seemed to be humorously saying, 'wait. I
know, my dear fellow, you are getting fidgety; but wait — and
we shall enjoy together the wild pleasure of discovering what
"Henry James" thinks of this matter. For my part, I dare not hurry
him!' . . .

I remember the first time I met him (the occasion was an
evening party) I asked him if he thought London 'beautiful' — an
idiotic question; worse than that, a question to which I did not
really want an answer, though there were hundreds of others
(some no doubt also idiotic) which I was longing to ask. But it
worked. To my dismay it worked only too well. 'London? Beautiful?' he began, with that considering slant of his massive head I
was to come to know so well, his lips a little ironically compressed, as though he wished to keep from smiling too obviously.
'No: hardly beautiful. It is too chaotic, too —' then followed

a discourse upon London and the kind of appeal it made to the historic sense, even when it starved the aesthetic, which I failed to follow; so dismayed was I at having, by my idiot's question, set his mind working at such a pitch of concentration on a topic indifferent to me . . . At the end of a sentence, the drift of which had escaped me but which closed, I think, with the words 'find oneself craving for a whiff of London's carboniferous damp', I did however interrupt him. Enthusiasm and questions (the latter regarding *The Awkward Age* [1899], just out) poured from my lips. A look of bewilderment, almost of shock, floated for a moment over his fine, large, watchful, shaven face, on which the lines were so lightly etched. For a second he opened his rather prominent hazel eyes a shade wider, an expansion of the eyelids that to my imagination seemed like the adjustment at me of the lens of a microscope; then the great engine was slowly reversed, and a trifle grimly, yet ever so kindly, and with many reassuring pats upon the arm, he said: 'I understand, my dear boy, what you mean — and I thank you.' (Ouf! What a relief!)

He went on to speak of *The Awkward Age*. 'Flat' was, it appeared, too mild an expression to describe its reception. 'My books make no more sound or ripple now than if I dropped them one after the other into the mud.' And he had, I learnt to my astonishment, in writing that searching diagnosis of sophisticated relations, conceived himself to be following in the footsteps, 'of course, with a difference', of the sprightly Gyp![1] Hastily and emphatically I assured him that where I came from, at Cambridge, his books were very far from making no ripple in people's minds. At this he showed some pleasure; but I noticed then, as often afterwards, that he was on his guard against being gratified by appreciation from any quarter. He liked it — everybody does, but he was exceedingly sceptical about its value. I doubt if he believed that anybody thoroughly understood what, as an artist, he was after, or how skilfully he had manipulated his themes; and speaking with some confidence for the majority of his enthusiastic readers at that time, I may say he was right.

[1] 'The ingenious and inexhaustible, the charming philosophic "Gyp".' H. J., Introduction to *The Awkward Age* (1908).

He was fully aware of his idiosyncrasy in magnifying the minute. I remember a conversation in a four-wheeler ('the philosopher's preference' he called it) about the married life of the Carlyles. He had been re-reading Froude's *Life of Carlyle*, and after remarking that he thought Carlyle perhaps the best of English letter-writers he went on to commiserate Mrs Carlyle on her dull, drudging life. I protested against 'dull', and suggested she had at least acquired from her husband one source of permanent consolation and entertainment, namely the art of mountaining mole-hills. A look of droll sagacity came over his face, and turning sideways to fix me better and to make sure I grasped the implication, he said: 'Ah! but for that, where would *any of us* be?'

Desmond MacCarthy

Quest for Perfection

[Many raconteurs anxious to recall the true accents of the Master have represented him as, in his hesitations, groping for phrases and varying them in mid-sentence. An example is quoted from W. G. Elliot on page 87 below. The following passage provides an instructive commentary on recollections of that type.]

His habit of hemming and hawing . . . was largely due to . . . shyness. I had originally diagnosed it . . . as a quest for perfection: instinctively bringing out the perfect sentence the first time; repeating it more deliberately to test every word the second time; accepting it as satisfactory the third time, and triumphantly sending it forth as produced by Henry James. One example of this has been a feature of my intimate monologues ever since. I can still produce it word for word, with the exact timing and every intonation of Henry's voice . . .

I had asked Mr James if he himself accepted literally Mr Landor's recital of his incredible experiences in Tibet.[1] Mr James reflected an instant over this problem and then delivered his verdict.

---

[1] *In the Forbidden Land*, by A. Henry Savage Landor (1898). A haplography in James's comment as printed in *Three Rousing Cheers* has here been remedied by collation of the version which Miss Jordan later gave to the *Mark Twain Quarterly*.

'Eliminating — ah —' he said, 'eliminating, ah-h — eliminating nine-tenths — nine-tenths — nine-*tenths*(slowly) — of-of-of (very fast) — of what he claims — what he claims (slowly) — what he claims (very slow) — there is still (fast) — there — is still — there is still (faster) — enough left (pause) enough left (pause) to make — to make — to make (very fast) a remarkable record (slow) — a remarkable record — ah — ah — (slower) — a re-markable re-cord!'

There is no exaggeration in that quotation. It is a typical example of Mr James's ordinary method of speech. He almost never changed a word in his verbal gropings, and the intelligent reader will observe that every word in the sentence was the word which best expressed Mr James's meaning. And (as always) those seemingly fumbling, groping phrases held, when complete, deep food for reflection.

I soon learned, however, that when Mr James was deeply interested these little affectations of speech fell away. He spoke always with rare and exquisite use of words as the tools of his trade: but he talked naturally and simply, and often with beguiling humour and an odd exuberance.

Elizabeth Jordan

H. J. AS LINGUIST

In an Italian Villa

[In 1899 James spent 'four or five picturesquissimo' days at the Humphry Wards' villa at Castel Gandolfo where Mrs Ward was writing 'an "Italian" novel'. When later returning the proofs of *Eleanor* he asked whether a particularly odious minor character was 'by the way, naturally — as it were — H. J.???!!!' In fact the only use which Mrs Ward appears to have made of H. J. in *Eleanor* was in describing a visit paid together to Nemi and in portraying, under the name that had greatly attracted H. J., a boy called Aristodemo.]

Never did I see Henry James in happier light. A new light too. For here in this Italian country, and in the Eternal City, the man whom I had so far mainly known as a Londoner was far more at home than I; and I realized perhaps more fully than ever before the extraordinary range of his knowledge and sympathies.

Roman history and antiquities, Italian art, Renaissance sculpture, the personalities and events of the Risorgimento, all these solid *connaissances* and many more were to be recognized perpetually as rich elements in the general wealth of Mr James's mind. That he had read immensely, observed immensely, talked immensely, became once more gradually and delightfully clear on this new field. That he spoke French to perfection was of course quickly evident to anyone who had even a slight acquaintance with him. M. Bourget once gave me a wonderful illustration of it. He said that Mr James was staying with himself and Madame Bourget at their villa at Hyères, not long after the appearance of Kipling's *Seven Seas*. M. Bourget, who by that time read and spoke English fluently, complained of Mr Kipling's technicalities, and declared that he could not make head or tail of McAndrew's Hymn. Whereupon Mr James took up the book, and standing by the fire, fronting his hosts, there and then put McAndrew's Hymn into vigorous idiomatic French — an extraordinary feat, as it seemed to M. Bourget . . .

But Mr James was also very much at home in Italian, while in the literature, history and art of both countries he moved with the well-earned sureness of foot of the student. Yet how little one ever thought of him as a student! That was the spell. He wore his learning — and in certain directions he was learned — 'lightly, like a flower' . . . His knowledge was conveyed by suggestion, by the adroitest of hints and indirect approaches. He was politely certain, to begin with, that you knew it all; then to talk *with you* round and round the subject, turning it inside out, playing with it, making mock of it, and catching it again with a sudden grip, or a momentary flash of eloquence, seemed to be for the moment his business in life. How the thing emerged, after a few minutes, from the long involved sentences! — only involved because the impressions of a man of genius are so many, and the resources of speech so limited. This involution, this deliberation in attack, this slowness of approach towards a point which in the end was generally triumphantly rushed, always seemed to me more effective as Mr James used it in speech than as he employed it — some of us would say to excess — in a few of his latest books. For in talk his own living personality — his flashes of fun, of courtesy, of 'chaff' — were always there, to do away with what, in the written word, became a difficult strain on attention.

I remember an amusing instance of it when my daughter D——, who was housekeeping for us at Castel Gandolfo, asked his opinion as to how to deal with the Neapolitan cook, who had been anything but satisfactory, in the case of a luncheon-party of friends from Rome. It was decided to write a letter to the ex-bandit in the kitchen, at the bottom of the fifty-two steps, requesting him to do his best and pointing out recent shortcomings. D——, whose Italian was then rudimentary, brought the letter to Mr James, and he walked up and down the vast *salone* of the villa, striking his forehead, correcting and improvising. 'A really nice pudding' was what we justly desired, since the Neapolitan genius for sweets is well known. Mr James threw out half phrases — pursued them — improved upon them — withdrew them — till finally he rushed upon the magnificent bathos, 'un dolce come si deve!' — which has ever since been the word with us for the tip-top thing.

Mrs Humphry Ward

Mastery of French

James's simple cordiality would have made him welcome anywhere; but he was particularly popular among his French friends, not only on account of his quickness and adaptability, but because his youthful frequentations in the French world of letters, following on the school-years in Geneva, had so steeped him in continental culture that the cautious and inhospitable French intelligence felt at once at ease with him. This feeling was increased by his mastery of the language. French people have told me that they had never met an Anglo-Saxon who spoke French like James; not only correctly and fluently, but — well, just as they did themselves; avoiding alike platitudes and pomposity and using the language as spontaneously as if it were his own.

Edith Wharton

Even those [among the cast of *The American*] who had little French of their own felt that Mr James's reflected distinction on the enterprise. Certainly we had not heard anything comparable in other theatres. Someone — and I do wish I could be sure who — enlightened the rest of us as to the 'suppleness' of our author's linguistic equipment. 'When he talks to George Moore — it is the French of the Academy. When he talks to Miss Dairolles (the "Noémie" of our cast) it is French of the *coulisses*.' We felt, to be talked to as if you were a member of the Français gave Adrienne Dairolles an unfair advantage.

Elizabeth Robins

French with Tears

[James wrote to his French correspondents sometimes in English, sometimes in French. To Auguste Monod, the translator of some of his books, he once wrote of '*les Deux Magiques*' (*sic*) — of which Monod remarked that it was '*un des cas très rares où Henry James se trompe de mot en Français*'.[1]]

I make no apology for addressing you in the most economic of our several familiar idioms; by which I mean that to write in French is, to me, though feasible after a fashion, an enterprise requiring time and space, prayer and meditation, a dictionary, a grammar, a phrase-book, an extra supply of ink and paper, and last not least, an infinite charity on the part of my victim.

H. J. to J.-E. Blanche, 1908

READING ALOUD

One night some one alluded to Emily Brontë's poems and I said I had never read 'Remembrance'. Immediately he took the volume from my hand and, his eyes filling, and some far-away emotion deepening his rich and flexible voice, he began . . .

[1] The correct French for *The Two Magics* could be *Les Deux Magies*: '*magique*' is adjectival.

I had never before heard poetry read as he read it; and I never have since. He chanted it, and he was not afraid to chant it, as many good readers are, who, though they instinctively feel that the genius of the English poetical idiom requires it to be spoken *as poetry*, are yet afraid of yielding to their instinct because the present-day fashion is to chatter high verse as though it were collo-quial prose. James on the contrary, far from shirking the rhythmic emphasis, gave it full expression. His stammer ceased as by magic as soon as he began to read, and his ear, so sensitive to the convolutions of an intricate prose style, never allowed him to falter over the most complex prosody but swept him forward on great rollers of sound till the full weight of his voice fell on the last cadence.

James's reading was a thing apart, an emanation of his inmost self, unaffected by fashion or elocutionary artifice. He read from his soul, and no one who never heard him read poetry knows what that soul was. Another day some one spoke of Whitman, and it was a joy to me to discover that James thought him, as I did, the greatest of American poets. *Leaves of Grass* was put into his hands, and all that evening we sat rapt while he wandered from 'The Song of Myself' to 'When lilacs last in the door-yard bloomed' (when he read 'Lovely and soothing Death' his voice filled the hushed room like an organ adagio), and thence let himself be lured on to the mysterious music of 'Out of the Cradle', reading, or rather crooning it in a mood of subdued ecstasy till the fivefold invoca-tion to Death tolled out like the knocks in the opening bars of the Fifth Symphony.

Edith Wharton

TELEGRAMS

Accepting an Invitation

Will alight precipitately at 5.38 from the deliberate 1.50.

H. J. to Edwin Abbey

Refusing an Invitation

Impossible impossible impossible if you knew what it costs me to say so you can count however at the regular rates ask Miss Robins to share your regret I mean mine.

H. J. to Mrs Hugh Bell

SOCIAL OCCASIONS

MANNERS OF THE VICTORIANS

The Siege of Society

When I happened to speak with some disapprobation of the pursuit by Americans of social success in London in spite of the rudeness encountered from some of the London social leaders he said: 'I don't agree with you. I think a position in society is a legitimate object of ambition.'

E. S. Nadal

Mr R.[1] is extremely sensitive, and he asked H. once how often he had been obliged to leave country houses suddenly because he had been uncivilly treated therein. When H. said he had never done such a thing he seemed greatly surprised and said, 'Sometimes I have gone off in the baker's cart.'

Alice James, 1889

Class Distinctions

I would often go to see him [at 3 Bolton Street in 1877]. There was a slender, tall, dark, rather pretty girl who usually came to the door when I called. She was not a servant but a relation of the landlady. James, with his quick sympathy and the keen interest he had lately acquired in English habits, said: 'She's an English

[1] George W. E. Russell, grandson of the sixth Duke of Bedford, journalist, politician, who later became a Privy Councillor and Under-Secretary for the Home Department.

character. She is what they call in England a "person". She isn't a lady and she isn't a woman; she's a person.' . . .

In the things he wrote about that time I could see indications that his personal relations with English society were very much in his mind. In 'An International Episode' an American woman says that an English woman had said to her, 'In one's own class,' meaning the middle class and meaning also that the American woman belonged to that class. The American woman says that she didn't see what right the English woman had to talk to her in that manner.[1] This was a transcript of an incident he related to me one night when we were walking about the London streets. Some lady of the English middle class whom he had lately visited in the country had said to him, 'That is true of the aristocracy, but in one's own class it is different,' meaning, said James, 'her class and mine'. He did not wish to be confounded with the mass of English people and to be adjudged a place in English society in accordance with English standards.

E. S. Nadal

Ostentation (American)

There is an account of a wedding in the *Standard* of some New Yorkers. Three presents are mentioned: 'A golden dinner-service from an uncle, a golden dessert-service from a brother, and a book from Lady Something Thynne' — how thin it *do* sound. Can you imagine anything so vulgar as the gold? The bride, instead of a bouquet, had a silver prayer-book in her hand. I told H., with disgust! to which he said: 'Surely a lady who can eat off gold ought to be able to pray out of silver!'

Alice James, 1890

---

[1] 'In one's own class of life! What is a poor unprotected American woman to do in a country where she is liable to have that sort of thing said to her?' — 'An International Episode' (1879), V.

Demoralization (British)

Harry came in the other day quite sickened from a conversation he had been listening to, which he said gave him a stronger impression of the demoralization of English society than anything he had ever heard. He had been calling upon a lady whom he knows very well, and who is very well connected; two gentlemen were there, one young, the other old; one of them asked about one of the sons who had just failed in an exam. for one of the services, when she said he had just had an offer of a place, their opinion of which she would like to have. Pulitzer, the ex-editor of the *New York World*, had applied to the British Embassy in Paris to recommend him a young man of good family to act as his secretary, write his letters, etc. — but chiefly to be socially useful in attracting people to the house; to act in short, evidently, as a decoy duck to Pulitzer's gilded salons. A certain young man had fulfilled the functions for three years and had just been married to an American, Pulitzer having given him a '*dot*' of 30,000 pounds, and it was presumable that his successor would fare equally well. The Englishmen both thought it would be a 'jolly' life. She then turned and asked H. what he thought. 'I would rather sweep the dirtiest crossing in London.'

Alice James, 1890

Marquis and Butler

Last autumn at the South Kensington Hotel nurse told me one day that the Marquis of Lorne had arrived the day before, that a fine suite of rooms had been prepared for him on the first floor, but that he had taken only one bedroom on the fourth floor, and hadn't brought even a valet with him; and instead of ringing the bell for a housemaid he went in an ancient dressing-gown to a room where they sat and there gave his orders. When this was told in the steward's room 'Mr' Woodford, the butler who presided over the deglutition of the ladies' maids, unctuous of manner, Pickwickian of contour, his legs behind him, his figure 'not lost but gone before', exclaimed, 'Oh, that's the real kind;

you soon tell 'em from the made-up ones.' How he would despise anyone not a marquis who behaved like that! H. says, 'It takes a marquis to make a butler subtle.'

Alice James, 1891

Poverty and Wealth

I was amazed, too, by his standard of decent comfort; and his remark on our leaving what appeared to me a thoroughly well-appointed, prosperous house, 'Poor S., poor S. — the stamp of unmistakable poverty upon everything!' has remained in my memory . . . His dislike of squalor was so great that surroundings to be tolerable to him had positively to proclaim its utter impossibility. 'I can stand,' he once said to me while we were waiting for our hostess in an exceptionally gilt and splendid drawing-room, 'a great deal of gold.'

The effects of wealth upon character and behaviour attracted him as a novelist, but no array of terms can do justice to his lack of interest in the making of money. He was at home in describing elderly Americans who had acquired it by means of some invisible flair, and on whom its acquisition had left no mark beyond perhaps a light refined fatigue (his interest in wealth was therefore the reverse of Balzacian); or in portraying people who had inherited it. Evidence of ancient riches gave him far more pleasure than lavishness, and there we sympathized; but above all the signs of tradition and of loving discrimination exercised over many years in conditions of security soothed and delighted him. Lamb House, his home at Rye, was a perfect shell for his sensibility. He was in the habit of speaking of its 'inconspicuous little charm', but its charm could hardly escape anyone; so quiet, dignified and *gemütlich* it was, within, without.

Desmond MacCarthy

THE DINER-OUT

Masked Ball

. . . a most amusing masked ball at [Hardy's] friends, Mr and Mrs Montagu Crackanthorpe's, where he and Henry James were the only two not in dominos, and were recklessly flirted with by the women in consequence.

Mrs Hardy

At the Gosses'

[The Edmund Gosses gave an annual New Year's Party.]

After seasonable refreshment downstairs the guests would be led to a not very large room at the top of the house for some form of entertainment — usually quite a good one, but this time our hosts had made an unlucky choice; and the literary lights of London, packed like figs in a box, observed with languor the performance of some third-rate marionettes. After a while Mr James, who was standing beside me squeezed against a wall, turned to me with a malicious gleam in his eye. 'An interesting example, my dear Marsh, of Economy — Economy of Means — and — and — and — ' (with an outburst) 'Economy of *Effect!*'

Edward Marsh

Table d'Hôte

Henry James . . . would regale us with accounts of the various dilemmas into which his shyness had precipitated him. On one occasion, at a table d'hôte on the Continent where he found himself in the centre of a long table, he felt very ill at ease until he had fortified himself with a bottle of claret. After a glass his spirits revived and he was just getting into his stride with the lady on his right and waving his hands about, as was his habit while talking, when to his horror he knocked over his bottle of wine which cascaded into the lady's lap. She was, however, most comforting and he ordered a second bottle. Gradually confidence returned and gesticulation sprang into abnormal activity. Suddenly a lady on the opposite side of the table, who had been practising her English on her neighbours, was heard to exclaim in a loud voice, 'Luke, luke, 'e 'ave done it again!' And sure enough the same lady received a second deluge of claret. This was too much for James, who immediately retired to his room and left the hotel early next morning.

C. C. H. Millar

At the Russells'

Lady Arthur Russell, while her husband was alive, had regularly given parties on Tuesday evenings at her house in Audley Square. Henry James was one of the *habitués*, and he enjoyed going to see her on other days too, though he had been known to remark on the difficulty of making conversation 'under the eyes of that long row of silent, observant children'. When these same children grew up the 'Tuesdays' were revived, partly for their friends and partly for the survivors from the old days. I met him there on his first appearance, and he stood beside me, surveying the guests with 'no unpleasing melancholy'. 'It's a strange experience,' he said, 'to come back after all these years to the scene of so many memories — to find a few of the old familiar figures retired in the background, and the foreground filled with a mass of the portentous young, of whom, my dear Marsh,' (and here came the beam of eye and voice) 'you are one.' I think it was to Lady Arthur, who had asked him if he knew the names of woman's clothes, that he answered: 'I know a bertha — and a spencer — and a ruff.'

Edward Marsh

No More Dinners

[During the winter of 1878–9 James, by his own account, dined out 107 times. He was still hard at it in 1895.]

Don't think me a monster of unsociability, of unfriendship, if I tell you the truth on the question of accepting your hospitable invitation for Monday. The great dining-out business has lately reached a point with me at which I have felt that something must be done — that I must in other words pull up. I have been doing it nightly ever since Nov. 1st, and it has left me with such arrears of occupation on my hands that it is imperative for me to try and use a few evenings to catch up. I am therefore accepting no invitations for the present — having got all the last but one well behind me. This is the plain unvarnished tale that I let loose at you instead of gracefully romancing about another engagement. Alas — 'alas' is hypocritical! what I *really* mean is that I can never dine out any more at all! It has come to the question of that or leaving London, and I must try that first. It is heroic and really tests me, to have to take you so early in the period.

H. J. to S. Colvin, 26 December 1895

Howells-and-James

There was a time when Mr James and Mr Howells used to be bracketed, as if they hunted in couples; which was not a discriminating view though a popular view. It expressed itself in the jingle about 'Howells and James Young Men', of which the music hall was the proper home;[1] and there it related to a firm in Regent Street, now extinct. But it was sung by the daughters of a house where Mr James was a guest, and almost in his hearing, to the horror of its mistress.

G. W. Smalley

[1] In Gilbert's *Patience*, 1881, the 'Howell [sic] and James young man' is the antithesis of the 'greenery-yallery, Grosvenor Gallery' aesthete. Nevertheless James's connection with the Grosvenor Gallery set and his friendship with W. D. Howells, then the leading literary light of Boston, made the perversion of the jingle inevitable. A year or two after *Patience* Henry Adams was writing of 'our Howells and James epoch'. The young Hamlin Garland when he first went to Boston found that 'the critics and reviewers invariably alluded to "Howells and James" as if they were some sort of firm, or at least literary twins', and he formed a prejudice against the firm before he had read either of them. Arthur Symons in the 'nineties coupled them as the 'heads of the very modern school of story-telling which considers it unbecoming to have any story to tell'. But this, as Smalley says above, and as

An Appreciated Guest

[In 1885 James paid many short visits, and one of several weeks, to Bournemouth in order to be with his invalid sister. He frequented Skerryvore, the Stevensons' house, which once he found over-full of guests. He wrote: 'My visit had the gilt taken off by the somewhat ponderous presence of (R.L.S.'s) parents — who sit on him much too long at once.']

It has been such a difficult party that I quite broke down under the strain. Through it all the dear Henry James remained faithful, though he suffered bitterly and openly. He is gone now and there is none to take his place. After ten weeks of Henry James the evenings seem very empty, though the room is always full of people.

Mrs R. L. Stevenson, 1885

A Tactful Guest

Poor old Godkin had had a stroke. At breakfast H. J. made some ordinary remark — 'Pass me the butter', perhaps. Godkin thought it a joke and laughed aloud. H. J. at first was puzzled; then (and it was one of the nicest things I ever saw) began to smile as if hesitating to laugh at his own wit, and finally joined in Godkin's hearty laugh. It made a great impression on me.

Henry Dwight Sedgwick

CLUB, STUDIO AND SALON

At that time [1877–8] he was rather keen upon the subject of English clubs. He liked them and wanted to become a member of one or two of them. He had his name put up for the Reform. He had no difficulty in obtaining an election, but of course one can never be quite sure of getting into a club. I remember his saying

Garland soon read enough to learn, is an undiscriminating view. George Moore, discriminating and epigrammatic, remarked that Henry James came to Europe and studied Turgenev while Howells remained in America and studied Henry James.

to me: 'If I should fail in this I shall then go to work and write some things and try to get an election to the Athenaeum.' He meant an election under the rule of that club which permits the choice annually of a certian number of men who have become distinguished in politics, literature, science or the fine arts. He said that he had already certain friends in that club who were taking care of him.

E. S. Nadal[1]

At the Reform

. . . Il prenait une chambre au Reform-Club. Je lunchais avec lui dans l'une des salles de cet énorme cercle politique, parlementaire, point 'chic' du tout, mais l'un des plus majestueux palais palladiens de Pall-Mall. Il semblait y passer inaperçu, la gloire ne l'entourait pas d'une auréole . . . Henry redoutait le domestique qui lui remettrait une carte de visite. Aurait-on appris sa présence en ville? Qu'il connût ou non le visiteur, James se disposait à lui faire répondre: 'Mr Henry James est sorti.' C'est ainsi qu'une fois il avait refusé de recevoir certain porteur d'un manuscrit, et qui n'était autre que Joseph Conrad.

J.-E. Blanche

Ghosts

In the coffee-room of the Reform Club he came up to me and said: 'You probably don't remember me. I'm Henry James.' I blushed . . . He asked me if I was alone. I said I had two guests. He said: 'May I join your party upstairs?' I blushed again. It seemed to me

---

[1] It is difficult to accept the suggestion that James, when deciding to go to work and write some things, was actuated by his ambition to be elected to the Athenaeum. For the general tone of Nadal's reminiscences, however, see page 18 above.

James was a member of the Reform from 1878 until his death; he was elected to the Athenaeum under Rule II in 1882; he joined the Savile in 1884 but 'loved it not', rarely visited it and resigned in 1899.

incredible that Henry James should actually be asking to join my party. We received him with all the *empressement* that he desired. He talked. He did all the talking, and he was exceedingly interesting . . .

Hy. James said of Reform: 'This is for me now a club of ghosts. There were special corners and chairs. It is fuller, too, now than it used to be.' He also said that the club was built before clubs were fully understood, and he objected to largeness of atrium or cortile, making all rooms round it seem small. He described in full James Payn's daily life: — drove down from Maida Vale or somewhere to Smith Elder's, and left there before 1 in order to be at club at 1. Numberless friends. Amusing companion. Played whist, etc., every afternoon and got home (driving) about 7. Never walked. Never wanted other interests. No intellectual curiosity. Large family, but was not interested in it. I asked when he did his work: James said he certainly never worked either afternoon or night. He was continually politely sarcastic about Payn . . .

He told us about all the ghosts, one after another. There was no touch of sentimentality in his recollections. Everything was detached, just, passionless and a little severe — as became his age. His ghosts were the ghosts of dead men, and his judgments on them were no longer at the mercy of his affections.

Arnold Bennett[1]

In the Barber's Chair

I have no intention of recounting my various clubs, but the next was the Reform, out of which, so far as frequenting it was concerned, I was driven by Henry James. I liked him well, but I had discovered another thing you can do in clubs, you can get your hair cut there. I naturally clung to that, but alas James, who was a true frequenter, clung to it also, and when one is swaddled in that white cloth one wants no friendly neighbour. At such

---

[1] The second of the three paragraphs quoted is from Bennett's Journal for January 1914; the first and third from an account written some years later.

times he and I conversed amiably from our chairs with raging breasts. Then one day I was in Manchester or Liverpool in a big hotel, and it came to me that now was my chance to get my hair cut in peace. I went downstairs, and just as they enveloped me in the loathly sheet I heard a groan from the adjoining chair and saw that its occupant was Henry James. After a moment, when anything might have happened, we both laughed despairingly, but I think with a plucky sympathy, meaning that fate was too much for us. Later in the day we discussed the matter openly for the first time, but could come to no conclusion for future guidance. Each, however, without making any promise, did something to help. Feeling that I had been driven from society by its greatest ornament I let my hair go its own wild way, and he, though he remained in society, removed his beard, which was what had taken him so often to the salon of the artists. Not that I can claim the beard as a trophy of mine, but he did remove it about that time, and I should have been proud to be the shears, for the result was that at last his full face came into the open, and behold it was fair.

J. M. Barrie

Mr James's Hat

[Stephen Crane, Harold Frederic and Charles Griswold, all Americans, had dined one evening in February 1898 in Richmond, where they had been joined by an English nobleman and a lady of uncertain origins.]

The party came back to Mr Griswold's rooms in London, and Madame Zipango . . . was imitating Yvette Guilbert when Henry James appeared to pay his young campatriot a call. The correct and the incorrect swam together in a frightful collison. Crane withdrew the elderly novelist to a corner and talked style until the fantastic woman poured champagne in the top hat of Henry James. Her noble lover had gone to sleep. Frederic was amused. The wretched host of this group was too young and too frightened to do anything preventative, and Crane, coldly tactful, got the handsome creature out of the hotel, then came back to aid in the restoration of the absurd hat.

Crane did not find this funny. In the next week he wrote: 'I agree with you that Mr James has ridiculous traits, and lately I have seen him make a holy show of himself in a situation that — on my honour — would have been simple to an ordinary man. But it seems impossible to dislike him. He is so kind to everybody.'

Thomas Beer

A Hat for Mr Walpole

More significant now, on looking back, than any other small incident in our friendship I find the tiny adventure of the High Hat. In action this was all that it was. I had gone to the Reform Club — where for several years he kept rooms — to have luncheon with him. It was summer, and I was dressed in a light grey suit. After luncheon we went up to his room and after fumbling in a wardrobe he produced a large hat-box. Out of this came an extraordinary hat — the kind of hat that Mr Churchill used to wear before he took to bricklaying — almost a top hat but suddenly, at the summit, a bowler. It had a large curly brim, was exceedingly glossy and was lined with bright red silk. Allowing himself even more elaboration than usual he explained to me that this hat was too small for him, had never been worn by anyone, was surely destined for a wise and elegant head, had in it every kind of suggestion of glory and promise and summer weather and success, was miserable and ashamed by its long imprisonment in the wardrobe, had made him for many weeks self-conscious and unhappy because he neglected it, was gifted no doubt with some especial power of conveying wisdom and brilliance to the head that it crowned, was constructed by the best hatter in London — in fine, there was no hat like it and I — I alone — must wear it!

I blushed, I stammered, I conveyed my thanks. It was jolly of him to give it me, but I had already plenty of hats, nor would this fit me very well, and its shape — surely its shape was a little *odd* for the correct and London young man that I fancied myself to be!

But I thanked him. It was impossible, seeing him standing there, his stocky legs a little apart, his exciting, clean-shaven face gently (a little ironically?) smiling, *not* to be grateful at his pleasure. Yes, I thanked him and intimated that I would carry it away with me to Chelsea. Carry it away with me to Chelsea? Not at all. I must wear it now. He must see how I looked in it. My present hat should be sent to Chelsea by Special Messenger. Indeed, indeed I did not want to walk home in it. With my elegant grey suit this hat would look most absurd. I had, like any other proper young Englishman, a horror of appearing unusual. I would be sure to meet a friend. The friend would talk. I would be the mock of those literary circles that, alas, loved only too dearly any opportunity for mockery. I suggested, I hinted . . . James was kind, he was affectionate, but he was firm. He must see how I looked, he must see me down the street . . .

See me down the street he did, all down [Pall] Mall, watching from the portals of the Reform, his eyes beaming kindliness, his hands raised in gesture of benediction. At the end of [Pall] Mall I met Mrs Wanda Lawes, that most inveterate of literary gossips. In St James's Street, crimson of countenance, I buried myself in a cab.

I thought then only of his kindliness, his beneficence, his generosity. But now, in retrospect, was there not perhaps a test of my young snobbery, a hint — for me to catch if I were smart enough — at the need for some new adjustment of values? I still have The Hat. Last year I wore it at a wedding. At forty-eight it becomes me strangely. Was that also what he intended?

Hugh Walpole

Mrs Draper's Hat

[For her first meeting with James Mrs Wharton put on her newest dress, for the second a new hat. Neither made any impression on him: when, years later, they came to know one another well he could not recollect either meeting. Mrs Draper's experience was different.]

At Mrs Napier's house one day in 1913 I met Henry James . . . As I pulled myself up and away from his side, fascinated, exhausted and adoring, his eyes travelled up from under the corniced eyebrows and saw my hat. It was a small white satin affair, with a

cluster of tiny white love birds perched at the front. He gasped with
horror, pointed his finger and said with utter kindness, 'My child
. . . my very dear child — the cruelty — ah! the cruelty of your
hat! That once living — indeed yes, loving — creatures should
have been so cruelly separated by death to become so unhappily
and yet, ah! how becomingly united on your hat.'

Muriel Draper

At Sargent's

On one wall of [Sargent's] big room hung the 'Portrait of Mlle. X',
now placed at the end of one of the galleries of the Metropolitan
Museum. Dear Henry James, sitting beside me one night at
Sargent's house, began telling me the story of the infuriated
mother of 'Mlle. X' who had returned the portrait, not exactly post-
haste but as fast as so large a canvas could be returned, with a note
in which she expressed her outrage that so great an artist should
have made a *'portrait lubrique de ma fille'*. Dear James was
explaining that 'the dress, you see, cut a little perhaps generously,
and held by such slender promises of modesty across her shoulders'
. . . was upsetting to the good lady her mother, when he observed
that my own frock was held in place by nothing more than two
strands of blue pearls, one on each shoulder. In extreme agitation
lest I should pursue the analogy he launched into the most elaborate discussion and comparison of clothes then and 'now',
plunging further and further in his desire to free my mind of any
disapproving conclusion. His antics were endearingly elaborate,
but his entanglement became so complex that I finally extricated
him by saying, 'I think it must have been the face she objected
to.'

Muriel Draper

In a Paris Studio

Je ne puis oublier son humeur, ou joviale ou morose, la critique
désopilante des caractères où il se risqua dans l'intimité de mon

atelier, pendant les séances qu'il m'accorda vers 1905.[1] Je peignis
deux toiles: une étude, d'abord, où il se présentait de face, sous
l'aspect de moine bon vivant qu'il prenait parfois. Il sortait d'un
déjeuner, congestionné, se plaignant d'être trop bien nourri, trop
invité; après une maladie, il s'était astreint à un régime compre-
nant la lente mastication des aliments, dont il moquait la 'gymnas-
tique'; mais il avait foi en son régime. Les autres avaient achevé de
manger qu'il mâchait encore. On attendait qu'il donnât le signal du
départ, comme s'il eût été un roi. Alors il sucrait sa causticité de
compliments hyperboliques, d'excuses pour les convives, pigeons
et cailles sur lesquels tombait son regard d'épervier. Je me rapelle
qu'il comparait alors son nouveau système d'élaboration littér-
aire à cette mastication que prescrivait le docteur aux dyspeptiq-
ues: 'Fait-le tourner dans votre palais cent fois, avant d'avaler un
morceau de viande, pour qu'il s'assimile à l'organisme.' Mais 'les
scrupules du styliste et du penseur,' ajoutait-il en riant, 'ne l'en-
richissent point.' . . .

Le prestige de son frère William, l'émule de Bergson, il s'en
disait heureux, approuvait que 'la gloire d'un aussi profond esprit'
obnubilât 'la fragile figure d'un conteur d'historiettes'. Nous
savons ce que valent ces déclarations-là. Ce frère qu'il aimait,
qu'il respectait, n'approuva jamais 'complètement' un roman de
Henry . . . Le cadet ayant annoncé à son aîné qu'un nouvel
ouvrage de lui allait paraître, William lui demanda si ce roman-là
serait enfin *pour lui*. Henry aurait répondu: 'J'espère bien que
non! Pas plus celui-là que les autres . . .'[2] 'Dear, dear William,'
s'exclamait James, 'il est si *incroyablement*, si *suprêmement*, si

---

[1] This should presumably be 1908.

[2] Cf. H.J. to William James, 23 November 1905: 'Let me say, dear William, that
I shall be greatly humiliated if you *do* like [*The Golden Bowl*], and thereby lump
it, in your affection, with things, of the current age, that I have heard you express
admiration for and that I would sooner descend to a dishonoured grave than have
written.' William's reply to this letter will be found in *Letters of William James*, II,
240. In a later letter, part of which is quoted above on page 17, William criti-
cizes his brother's 'third manner' and imagines exasperated readers exclaiming:
'Say it *out*, for God's sake, and have done with it.' This he could write to a brother
about that brother's writing. But Peter Dunne ('Mr Dooley') could not at his first
meeting with the Master say to his face what he later confided to Mrs Wharton:
'Everything he said was so splendid — but I felt like telling him all the time: "Just
'pit it right up into Popper's hand".'

super-humainement, si *magnifiquement* spiritualiste! Laissons-le voguer dans les régions transcendantales de la pensée, au-dessus de nous, *poor, poor miserable human beings* (nous, pauvres, pauvres misérables créatures) attachées à la matière! . . .' D'une voix plaintive et flûtée, entrecoupée de soupirs, Henry me répétait ces paroles avec des hochements risibles de la tête, de grasses mains à la Renan simulant le geste sacerdotal de bénir:

'*Well, my good friend*, j'ai peur d'être bien bavard, un détestable modèle, je vous donne beaucoup de mal? Merci de votre *trop admirable* complaisance de fixer avec vos brosses *incomparables* mes traits *décadents*! Ne bougeons plus!'

Et il se remettait en position, pur recommencer, après quelques minutes, à parler: 'Je vous envie! Horreur d'écrire! Ecrire? Oh! combien votre art est plus direct que le nôtre!' . . .

Cette première étude, de face, que j'avais peinte rapidement, lui déplut autant qu'elle me satisfaisait peu. Il ne me dit pas, comme certain grand statuaire français: 'Je veux être représenté sublime'; mais je sentis qu'il ne lui aurait pas déplu de l'être comme un Gladstone, un *Prime minister*, fût-ce l'Honorable Mr Balfour, qui n'était pas encore pair du Royaume. Mon deuxième portrait, le profil dont les lettres de Henry James[1] nous font croire qu'il fut aussi enchanté que le premier l'avait attristé, pourtant je l'exécutai à l'aide de dessins stylisés, de photographies prises chez moi selon ses désirs; pose cherchée, discutée sans fin; c'est un poète-lauréat, au regard méditatif, lointain, se détachant sur un papier de William Morris à grappes de raisins et feuilles de vignes, dorées comme dans le cabinet d'un *don* d'Oxford ou de Cambridge. Toute la fantaisie que je me suis permise, et qui le ravit, ce fut de lui mettre un gilet chamois qu'il n'aurait plus osé porter, à son âge. Je savais, tout en le contentant, lui et ses admiratrices, ne pas m'éloigner de la ressemblance, ou de la vraisemblance morale, et même l'accentuer.

J.-E. Blanche

[1] H. J. to Ellen Emmet, 2 November 1908. The second canvas was exhibited at the New Gallery in London in November 1908. James wrote: 'The "funny thing about it" is that whereas I sat in almost full face, and left it on the canvas in that bloated aspect when I quitted Paris in June, it is now a splendid Profile, and with the body (and *more* of the body) in a quite different attitude; a wonderful *tour de force* . . . — consisting

Ambushed

The children of one of these admirers[2] longed to hear Henry
James at their mother's house, and to see the author of *What
Maisie Knew*. Without telling him I arranged an innocent
ambush. At tea-time James appeared and the compliments he
paid Mrs S. N. were in the most exaggerated Henry James
manner, even more so than I could possibly have promised the
younger members of the family, who were hidden behind a
screen. They were hard put to restrain the torrent of their mirth,
and though the sounds were exceedingly muffled I recognized the
voices of these rogues. Following that event, and for years after,
when one of them imitated Henry James there were snorts and
puffs and heavy breathing in their attempt to find the monu-
mental word — but that word never came.

Knowing nothing or very little about our hostess, and
imagining her quite other than she actually was, James set himself
to charm her by developing an abracadabral theory about Paris
stores; the dresses and fashions were described with a bravura
and a flaunting of the floral ornaments and patchouli of the
Second Empire. When I wanted to lead him back to literature he
shook his head to give me to understand that this was not the
right place — for when he came in he had made up his mind that
he was with business people who had no comprehension of the
artist's troubles and anxieties.

J.-E. Blanche

of course of his having begun the whole thing afresh on a new canvas after I had
gone, and worked out the profile, in my absence, by the aid of a fond memory
("secret notes" on my silhouette, he also says, surreptitiously taken by him) and
several photographs (also secretly) taken at that angle while I sat there with my
whole beauty, as I supposed, turned on. The result is wonderfully "fine" (for
me) — *considering!*'

The extract from Blanche is taken from *Mes Modèles* (1928). In his later book,
Portraits of a Lifetime (1937), Blanche shows himself touchily upset by James's
'extraordinary joke' and retaliates by what he appears to suppose to be a
damaging revelation of James's attitude, behind her back, to Mrs Wharton. But
Blanche's own slate is not wholly clean, as the 'innocent ambush' described in the
next extract may suggest.

[2] 'Certain women of fashion who were unknown to him.' The admirer in
question appears to have been Mrs Saxton Noble.

Musical Evening

Thibaud, Casals, Rubinstein, Kochanski and Szymanowski
were to be the nucleus of an evening at Edith Grove; so I sent a
line to Henry James informing him of this and begging him to join
us. He arrived early and sledged down the stairs into the room
with that extraordinary density of movement that was characteristic of him. He did not give the impression of putting one foot
before the other in order to carry his torso and its appendages
into the room. He came in all at once. Head, shoulders, arms,
body, legs arrived at the same time, inexorably displacing space
and leaving an almost visible vacancy in his wake. Solid
purposeful wholeness impelled him. All of him was there,
nothing left behind.

He sat quietly on the sofa beside me and awaited silently the
first notes of the Brahms B major piano trio which was to begin
the evening's programme. As the music progressed and the
incomparable tone of Casals's 'cello was heard in the short solo
passage of the first movement, his solemnly searching eyes
fastened on Casals's face and he seemed to listen by seeing. When
Thibaud began the brilliant passage for violin in the second
movement his eyes left Casals, as if he had drunk him all in
through his organs of sight — music, hands, bowing and all —
and centred on Thibaud, whom he watched with meticulous care
during the whole second movement. During the last, when
Arthur Rubinstein was burning the music out of the piano with
an accumulating speed that left even those great artists somewhat
breathless as he rushed them up to the high climax of the trio,
H. J. turned the attention of his listening eyes toward him and
kept it there until the performance came to a close. Only then did
he begin to question me and greet one or two of the artists as they
came up. His need for exhaustive analysis of each one separately
made it difficult for him to take them in collectively, and I left him
talking tortuous French to Thibaud . . .

Toward the end of the [Schubert] octet Montague Vert
Chester, in a new pair of white gloves, came into the room. As
was the unvarying custom at Edith Grove he crept into the
nearest seat he could find without even a whisper of greeting and

listened with the rest. It happened to be a seat on the other side of James, and when the music was over I presented him. 'Chester, this is Mr James.' Chester with a scant nod, for he had no social grace, said, 'Good evening, Mr James,' and began to talk across him to me. Knowing that Chester admired his works with an enthusiasm that he rarely accorded anything other than music, my son and pink food, I added, 'Mr Henry James, Chester.' He bounded up from his seat and shouted with excitement:

'What, not *the* Mr James? Not the great Henry James?' offering his white-gloved hand in clumsy respect, eyes popping from his head.

From under benevolent eyebrows *the* Mr James looked up and said soothingly, 'Take it gently, my good man, take it gently.'

Muriel Draper

At Mary Cholmondeley's

There was one friend of [Rhoda Broughton's], much beloved, whom it was ever a joy to see matched against her, Henry James. He admired Rhoda, he wondered at her as a piece of uncompromising Britishry; he liked her, but especially he liked her for being what she was, so authentic a block of character, a type so unqualified; and again he recoiled, he held up his hands in a horror of her barbarism — her slapdash cut-and-thrust at the questions and the issues that require so many a discrimination for any fitting exploration of whatever may be discernible as their last significance of implication. Rhoda came slashing into the argument as though it could be hacked in two, right and left, and a straight way laid open down the middle. 'Our dear Rhoda — our gallant and intrepid Rhoda — admirable, wonderful as she is in her dauntless valiance — our beloved Rhoda, as I say —' in short she destroyed the possibility of anything that could in any valid sense be described as talk — as talk. Rhoda loved him greatly, but feared him not at all; she welcomed him with delight, but she didn't cherish or spoil him; and she could disconcert him at times, what with her boldness of attack and her insensibility to the shades and the semi-tones and the fine degrees of civilized thought. It was beautiful to see them together, complicated cosmopolitanized America and barbarous old Britain; and Britain had the best of it, not earning or deserving the victory, by cheerful unawareness of defeat. The company drew round to watch; it was an encounter to be recalled with relish.

Look, for example: Henry James, massive in the centre, his great head thrown back, his wide and steady eye fixed upon the twining of his thought as he slowly uncoils it; his voice breaking out in sonority as his phrase is amplified, qualified, left suspended for an interlude, recovered and again developed; slowly, deliberately the argument is built and adorned; and you see the climax looming, you wait and wonder how he will shape its last enrichment. He talks of Shakespeare — of the portent of that brilliance, that prodigality, that consummation of the mind of the greatest of ages — all emerging out of what? — out of nothing, out of darkness, out of the thick provincial mud; from which a figure steps forth, a young man of ill condition, a lout from Stratford,[1] to reappear presently —

'A lout!' exclaimed Rhoda, 'me divine William a lout?'

'But wait, dear lady, wait — see where I'm coming out — he reappears, as I say, this lout from Stratford'——

'I *won't* have yer call me divine William a lout,' she cries; and that's flat; but still she mistakes his drift, the whole tendency of the contrast to exalt, to enhance the wonder of the transformation by which this — in short this——

You could as well resist the way of an ocean liner; Henry

---

[1] 'I am "a sort of" haunted by the conviction that the divine William is the biggest and most successful fraud ever practised on a patient world . . . I find it *almost* as impossible to conceive that Bacon wrote the plays as to conceive that the man from Stratford, as we know the man from Stratford, did.' — H. J. to V. Hunt, 1903.

'He talked to me in the church of Stratford of the inscrutable mystery of Shakespeare: the works on the one side, and on the other that dull face and all the stories we know of the man — "commonplace; commonplace; almost degrading".' — *John Bailey*, 1908.

For formal purposes, in James's introduction to *The Tempest* in the Renaissance Shakespeare, 1907, 'the lout from Stratford' became 'the transmuted young rustic'.

James, in the mighty momentum of his argument, is not to be deflected; the course of his phrase is shaped, he can't go back upon it now. 'In short, this *lout*——'

'I will *not* let yer call him a lout!' cries our dauntless, our relentless, our impossible Rhoda — who won't let go, won't see that she has missed the point, doesn't care if she has. 'Me beloved Jamie calling Shakespeare a lout!' — that's all she has to say, with a crackle of short laughter. O the ancient savagery, tout de même, of these islanders!

Percy Lubbock

STREET SCENES

London

We often dined at a club in Piccadilly to which I belonged. The season was over and there was nothing to do in the evening, and after dinner we would walk in the park or about the London streets. As we walked along James talked incessantly and with originality and somewhat of the authority of those who read aloud to you their thoughts out of their own minds. His talk was very alert and eager. I recall at the moment one or two incidents of those walks. A little street-walker begged of us. As he gave her something he said with feeling: 'They imitate so well the tones of wretchedness.' Again I remember his using the expression, 'This town which I adore.'

E. S. Nadal

An uncle of mine . . . once in the middle of Regent Street, crossing amongst the traffic, met James. Whilst they were standing there he learnt that my uncle had just returned from India. This struck him greatly, since he himself had just returned from what was to prove his last visit to America. He started to elaborate on the theme of the impression on an Englishman just returned from India made by an American living from many years in England who had just returned to England from a visit to his native land. It was impossible for many minutes to extricate him from the traffic.

Stephen Spender

Our occasional meetings were always a delight, even though his earnestness in matters of detail was sometimes an embarrassment. Once we left a dinner-party together, and after walking a little way hailed a hansom, in which I sat while he stood for several minutes on the footboard discussing with the cabman the route which would best meet our dual needs. In vain I murmured from within: 'Oh, Mr James, do tell him the Reform Club, and I'll go on from there'; still he unrolled his mental map of London, hatching alternative itineraries. On another occasion we were walking and talking down Pall Mall when for some special emphasis he turned half-left, pulling me round half-right to face him, and fixed me to the spot, with a hand on each shoulder, while we stood like a Siamese lighthouse amid the surge of pedestrians, and he tracked the *mot juste* through the maze of his large vocabulary.

Edward Marsh

[Wilson Steer was apt to worry about catching cold, and once returning home complained that:]

Henry James had kept him talking, dragging his words out as was his wont, at a street corner, and Steer was *inclined* to think the wind was East.

Mrs Evans

Funeral Procession

Walking uphill began to tire Henry James as his years increased, and he acquired the habit of stopping at particular points and carrying on his conversation face to face with his companion. It so happened that on a certain occasion he was in the funeral procession of a deceased local official. They were a large company marching two and two, he and a friend of mine — an occasional companion of his walks — being about the middle of the long column. On this solemn occasion, when on the road up to the cemetery they reached one of the spots where he was accustomed to halt and hold forth, an absent-minded fit seized him. He stopped as usual and turning round to his companion began an oration. Some dozen or more couples behind him, being thus brought to a standstill, were impatiently marking time while the foremost half of the column were marching on up the hill. His friend, not a little embarrassed, managed to hook the great man by the arm and gently slip out of the procession to take last place in the rear, which did not catch up with the main body till the cemetery was nearly reached.

A. G. Bradley

Laocoon

I was once walking with him and Mr John Galsworthy along the Rye Road to Winchelsea. His dachshund Maximilian ran sheep, so, not to curtail the animal's exercise, the Master had provided it with a leash at least ten yards long. Mr Galsworthy and I walked one on each side of James listening obediently whilst he talked. In order to round off an immense sentence the great man halted, just under Winchelsea Hill beneath the windows of acquaintances of us all. He planted his stick firmly into the ground and went on and on and on. Maximilian passed between our six legs again and again, threading his leash behind him. Mr Galsworthy and I stood silent. In any case we must have resembled the *Laocoon*, but when Maximilian had finished the resemblance must have been overwhelming. The Master finished his reflections, attempted to hurry on, found that impossible. Then we liberated ourselves with difficulty. He turned on me, his eyes fairly blazing, lifting his cane on high and slamming it into the ground: 'H . . .' he exclaimed, 'you are painfully young, but at no more than the age to which you have attained, the playing of such tricks is an imbecility! An im . . . be . . . cility!'

F. M. Hueffer

OUT-OF-DOORS

The Cockney

. . . drive to Borough Farm, heather bloom. Tea-party at door, outside, Mrs Humphry Ward, Mr Ward, Miss Sellars (tall and beautiful), and Mr Henry James. The Anglo-American Novelist had just arrived from London and was going back by a late train.

He described himself as an 'unmitigated Cockney', was surprised at the colour of the heather, and hearing ling spoken of, asked to look at it.

William Allingham, 1888

Town and Country

[Three letters, c. 1900.]

I am very homesick for town, and shall not again — between November and April — hibernate amid the pure elements. I pine for the sound of the buses and the colour of the jars at night in the chemists' windows . . .

I do [? so] wholly agree with you as to the preferability of London when nature is one waterspout that I quit it almost with tears even for so brief a period — it's the Ark in the Deluge . . .

Thanks for your good wishes in the matter of the ministrations of Pye Smith.[1] I *am* much better, mainly — but really think it less Pye than Rye, than, in short, the absence of Pie; i.e. the innocent country life, the no Dinners, the plain living and high thinking.

H. J. to Mrs Sitwell

[1 A distinguished Harley Street specialist.]

Motoring

James, who was a frequent companion on our English motor-trips, was firmly convinced that, because he lived in England and our chauffeur (an American) did not, it was necessary that the latter should be guided by him through the intricacies of the English country-side. Signposts were rare in England in those days, and for many years afterward . . .

It chanced however that Charles Cook, our faithful and skilful driver, was a born path-finder, while James's sense of direction was non-existent, or rather actively but always erroneously alert; and the consequences of his intervention were always bewildering and sometimes extremely fatiguing. The first time that my husband and I went to Lamb House by motor (coming from France) James, who had travelled to Folkestone by train to meet us, insisted on seating himself next to Cook on the plea that the roads across Romney marsh formed such a tangle that only an old inhabitant could guide us to Rye. The suggestion resulted in our turning around and around in our tracks till long after dark though Rye, conspicuous on its conical hill, was just ahead of us and Cook could easily have landed us there in time for tea.

Another year we had been motoring in the west country and on the way back were to spend a night at Malvern. As we approached (at the close of a dark rainy afternoon) I saw James growing restless and was not surprised to hear him say: 'My dear, I once spent a summer at Malvern and know it very well; and as it is rather difficult to find the way to the hotel, it might be well if Edward were to change places with me and let me sit beside Cook.' My husband of course acceded (though with doubt in his heart) and, James having taken his place, we awaited the result. Malvern, if I am not mistaken, is encircled by a sort of upper boulevard, of the kind called in Italy a *strada di circonvallazione*, and for an hour we circled about above the outspread city while James vainly tried to remember which particular street led down most directly to our hotel. At each corner (literally) he stopped the motor, and we heard a muttering, first confident and then anguished. 'This — this, my dear Cook, yes . . . this certainly is the right corner. But no; stay! A moment longer, please — in this light it's so difficult . . . appearances are so misleading . . . It may be . . . yes! I think it *is* the next turn . . . "a little farther lend thy guiding hand" . . . that is, drive on; but slowly, please, my dear Cook; *very* slowly!' And at the next corner the same agitated monologue would be repeated; till at length Cook, the mildest of men, interrupted gently: 'I guess any turn'll get us down into the town, Mr James, and after that I can ask' — and late, hungry and exhausted we arrived at length at our destination, James still convinced that the next turn would have been the right one if only we had been more patient.

The most absurd of these episodes occurred on another rainy evening when James and I chanced to arrive at Windsor long after dark. We must have been driven by a strange chauffeur — perhaps Cook was on a holiday; at any rate, having fallen into the lazy habit of trusting to him to know the way, I found myself at a loss to direct his substitute to the King's Road. While I was hesitating and peering out into the darkness James spied an ancient doddering man who had stopped in the rain to gaze at us. 'Wait a moment, my dear — I'll ask him where we are'; and leaning out he signalled to the spectator.

'My good man, if you'll be good enough to come here, please; a little nearer — so,' and as the old man came up: 'My friend, to put it to you in two words, this lady and I have just arrived here from *Slough*; that is to say, to be more strictly accurate, we have recently *passed through* Slough on our way here, having actually motored to Windsor from Rye, which was our point of departure; and the darkness having overtaken us, we should be much obliged if you would tell us where we now are in relation, say, to the High Street, which, as you of course know, leads to the Castle, after leaving on the left hand the turn down to the railway station.'

I was not surprised to have this extraordinary appeal met by silence and a dazed expression on the old wrinkled face at the window; nor to have James go on: 'In short' (his invariable prelude to a fresh series of explanatory ramifications), 'in short, my good man, what I want to put to you in a word is this: supposing we have already (as I have reason to think we have) driven past the turn down to the railway station (which in that case, by the way, would probably not have been on our left hand, but on our right), where are we now in relation to . . .'

'Oh, please,' I interrupted, feeling myself utterly unable to sit through another parenthesis, 'do ask him where the King's Road is.'

'Ah —? The King's Road? Just so! Quite right! Can you, as a matter of fact, my good man, tell us where, in relation to our present position, the King's Road exactly *is*?'

'Ye're in it,' said the aged face at the window.

Edith Wharton

Lost Again

After tea H. J. and I went for a walk . . . We crossed a moor and lost our way. A yokel came by. H. J. at some length, with difficulty adapting his language, asked our way. The yokel passed on and had gone ten yards when H. J. struck a posture — 'My name is Norval, on the Grampian hills . . .' came to my mind — strode at great strides across the intervening space, took a sixpence from his waistcoat pocket, handed it, in a fashion for an upper gallery to see, to the fellow. 'There, my man, put that in your pipe and smoke it.' I wanted to clap.

Henry Dwight Sedgwick

I shall never forget Henry James the novelist explaining to John Morley how he strayed off the road when visiting his brother William in Chocorua [in the wilds of New Hampshire]: 'I had been *lost* had not a peasant emerged from the wood with a bundle of faggots upon his shoulder and directed me to the Post.'

Bliss Perry

THEATRICALS

THE PROSCENIUM CLOCK

'Every dramatist, my dear Guthrie,' I remember his saying to me, 'and by "dramatist" I mean a writer who seriously attempts that most difficult and elusive art of expressing his impressions of life in a dramatic form — be that form Tragedy, Comedy, Melodrama or what you will — every dramatist, then, as he sits at his desk to evolve his conceptions, must first visualize, or have before his mental eye, the proscenium of a theatre. And above that proscenium an immense clock, its hands indicating the hour of eight-thirty. Those hands will move inexorably on, till they reach eleven, and that deplorably insufficient space of time is all that is allowed him in which to make the actions and motives, however intricate, of his dramatis personae intelligible to an audience which he dare not count upon as possessing more than the average degree of intelligence. In that busy period of two hours and a half — and even there I am considerably overstating it in omitting to deduct the time occupied by the two intervals, which may represent anything from twenty to thirty minutes — within two hours, then, he must present and solve the problem he has set himself, or he is doomed.'

F. Anstey (T. A. Guthrie)

[Henry James's first writings as a child in the 1850s had been dramatic. In 1869–72, in his early days of journalism, he contributed three short plays to American periodicals. His bibliographer, Le Roy Phillips, classifies these as farces, but Mr Edel says that they were presented *en tout sérieux* and finds in their sentiments and dialogue no shadow of an intention of farce or humour.

By the time of his visit to America in 1881–2 James had made a name as a novelist, particularly with 'Daisy Miller.' At the invitation of the

Madison Square theatre in New York he dramatized 'Daisy Miller' but the play though printed was not produced. Returning to London he tried it on the St. James's theatre, but with no greater success.

He seems then to have written no further plays until after the completion of his great theatrical novel *The Tragic Muse* towards the end of 1888. In the December of that year Edward Compton wrote to propose that James should dramatize *The American*. His first thought was to refuse, but having taken a week to think it over he acceded. From then on, for about five years, he devoted the greater part of his energies — and his hopes — to the theatre.]

THE AMERICAN

Author and Actor-Manager

Harry came on Thursday [8 May]. He had been to Chester to see the Comptons to make arrangements about *The American*. It is to be brought out in the provinces and acted there through the winter, and taken to London in the spring . . . The Comptons think very well of the play, and feel sure it will be a success; and they are much better judges of that than any one else, with their immense experience of audiences. H. was very much struck with their British decency and respectability, which was much revealed to him as he penetrated into their interior. Such a contrast to that of second-rate, or first-rate, for the matter of that, French actors, with whom prolonged personal intercourse would be simply impossible.

Alice James, 1890

In the autumn he went to Sheffield to read the play before it was put into rehearsal to the company that would perform it. The reading began at eleven o'clock and finished at a quarter to three.

'Well?' the author asked anxiously, when he and the actor-manager came out of the stage-door to take a short walk before dining together at half-past three, 'What was your impression, Compton?'

'It's too long,' said my father.

'Too long?' James repeated in courteous but distressed amazement.

'It took you three hours and three-quarters to read it and there are three intervals to allow for.'

'What shall we do?'

'We shall have to cut it.'

Henry James stopped dead and gazed at my father in agony. 'Cut it?' he gasped. 'Did you say "cut it"? But when we discussed the play you did not suggest it was too long.'

'No, it was not too long then. You've added at least forty pages to the script.'

'But here and there additions and modifications were necessary,' the author insisted.

Later on that afternoon my mother was able to prevail on Henry James to allow her to make suggestions for cuts, and that led to a formidable correspondence between them, much of it carried on by James in very long and elaborate telegrams offering to sacrifice a couple of 'that's' on one page . . .

On the evening of that day in Sheffield when Henry James read *The American* to the company he saw a performance of *The School for Scandal*. After the curtain had fallen he went round to my father's dressing room. For some minutes James sat in a contemplative silence. At last my father, in the way of the actor-manager, asked him how he had enjoyed Sheridan's comedy.

'A curious old play,' said Henry James slowly. 'A very curious old play,' he repeated in a tone that revealed his astonishment that such a play could still be put on the stage. And that was the only comment he made.

Compton Mackenzie

The Bed-Ridden Spectator

[7 January 1891] The great family event, over which I have been palpitating for the last eighteen months or more, has come off: *The American* was acted for the first time at Southport, which they call the Brighton of Liverpool, on 3 January, and seems to have been, as far as audience, Compton and author were concerned, a brilliant success. H. says that Compton [as Christopher Newman] acted admirably, and it was delightful to hear and see him (Harry) flushed with the triumph of his first ovation. At the end he was called for with great insistence, and was pushed on to the stage by the delighted and sympathetic company; at the third bow and round of applause Compton, who was standing with him, turned and seized both his hands and wrung them; very pretty of him, wasn't it? . . .

H. says that at about four o'clock he got so nervous that he couldn't eat any dinner, and went off to the theatre and walked about the stage, dusted the mantelpiece and set the pasteboard vases straight, turned down the corners of the rugs (after his usual manner in my apartments), when lo! as soon as the curtain went up, he became as calm as a clock . . .

William Archer, the dramatic critic of the *World* (who, Harry says, is far and away the best of his kind in London), wrote to Harry proposing to go to see the play at Southport. H. discouraged his doing so, on the ground of the distance and the cold, but he was there, notwithstanding, on Saturday night; and Harry, who had never met him before, was introduced to him in one of the entr'actes. After the play was over [Archer] told Balestier to tell Harrry that he wished to speak to him at the hotel. On returning, H. sent a message inviting him to his sitting-room. Upon his entrance Archer murmured some words of congratulations upon H.'s success, adding immediately: 'I think it's a play that would be much more likely to have success in the provinces than in London'; and then he began, as by divine mission, to enumerate all its defects and flaws, and asked why H. had done so-and-so, instead of the opposite, etc. To H., of course, heated from his triumph, these uncalled-for and depressing amenities from an entire stranger seemed highly grotesque; none the less so that to the eye, by his personal type (that of a dissenting minister), the young man seemed by nature divorced from all matters theatrical. In spite of the gloom cast over his spirits, H. was able to receive it all with perfect urbanity, and the Comptons etc. coming in to supper before long, he bowed Archer out, and served him up as a delectable dish of roast prig done to a turn[1] . . .

When you come upon these forms of existence, absolutely destitute of imagination and humour, can you wonder at the maddening irritation with which the critic fills the artist soul? — who, whatever he may not have done, has at least *attempted* to create. H. replies: 'Yes, but one is so inadequate for it, and would have to be a Frenchman to hate them enough and to express the irony, scorn and contempt with which one ought to be filled.' H., with his impervious mildness, certainly is inadequate to the subject, and remains completely unruffled by the whole fraternity.

[27 March] *The American* has been a great success in Belfast as well as in Edinburgh; there must be something human after all in Ulster!

[23 April] The Comptons also dwelt very much on the fact that, save a little excision, when they came to rehearse *The American* they had not suggested an alteration; this, it seems, is very unusual. Mrs Kendal says in her little book that plays have usually almost to be made over . . .

H. came in a few days ago, all heated with a most sympathetic interview with John Hare, who not only accepts play number two, *Mrs Vibert*, which H. wrote before Christmas for Miss Geneviève Ward, but accepts it with enthusiasm and calls it a 'masterpiece of dramatic construction'. His talk was most intelligent and his view of the English public all that can be desired. He talked a great deal about the cast, and repeated, 'It is meant for

---

[1] In a paragraph omitted here because Alice James told the story at fourth hand Archer is represented as having said to a friend that 'it was a most extraordinary and unheard of, almost immoral thing for a tyro to undertake to write a play without consulting a competent dramatic critic.'

Archer's notice in the *World* of the Southport production was not unfriendly but complained of 'a certain maladroitness of development'. His notice of the London production eight months later referred to his Southport visit and suggested that his fears had been confirmed (if not specifically that his advice had not been taken). 'There is a secret in dramatic writing as in every other art, and Mr James has not "guessed it first time".' Two months later again he saw the play once more and wrote 'Mr Henry James has rewritten the latter half of the third act of *The American* immensely to its advantage.'

the Français.' [Pinero's] *Lady Bountiful*, which he has just brought
out, has fortunately fallen, and he apparently would bring out
H.'s play now but that he wants, for a rest, to revive an old play,
and he has promised to bring out another new play next. So H.
won't come until the autumn or winter, I am afraid . . .

['*Mrs Vibert*' is the play later published as *Tenants*. In spite of Hare's
enthusiastic acceptance of it for the Garrick and of his holding it for
several years (to the inconvenience of the author), it was not put on.]

H. says that *Lady Bountiful* is put on the stage in the most
exquisite manner; the English surpass the French so enormously
in this way. I suggested that the French substitute the acting. 'Yes,
of course; here the acting is simply thrown in.' . . . H. said that,
whilst rehearsing with the Compton troupe, it was all very well to
be superior to the *mise-en-scène*, but with such inferior instru-
ments that it was an enormous support, and that he fell back
upon and 'clung to every button'.

[16 June] The difficulty with H.'s plays is going to be, according
to Hare, the absence of actors for them, their natural home being
the Français. I asked [H.] how he explained his suddenly finding
himself in possession of a dramatic construction so perfect. He
said that he had always felt sure he could write plays, but hated so
the process of hawking them about.

Within the last year he has published *The Tragic Muse*,
brought out *The American*, and written a play, *Mrs Vibert*
(which Hare accepted), and his admirable comedy; combined
with William's *Psychology*, not a bad show for one
family! — especially if I get myself dead, the hardest job of all.

This playing business is going to multiply H.'s benevolent
entanglements in a sad way. Besides the people from home whom
he visits, the sick and bereft perpetually renewed, whose hands
he holds, now all the dishevelled ladies come to him to set their
halting plays upon their legs, which amounts to his rewriting
them. Apropos of actresses, he says Miss Robins is the most
intelligent creature, next to Coquelin, with whom he ever talked
about her art.

Alice James, 1891

[For James's friendship with Elizabeth Robins, their common interest in Ibsen, his assistance to her over theatrical contracts and the revision of scripts, and in general for his interest in all aspects of the theatre in the 'nineties and later, see Miss Robins's book *Theatre and Friendship*.

In the London production of *The American* Miss Robins played the Comtesse de Cintré.]

Rehearsals

Apart from the acting — an exception he would have smiled at wryly, but I make it in all good faith — Mr James's enjoyment of those rehearsals was real enjoyment, at least while he was in the theatre.

I cannot think he ever felt the least strange there. Rather he was like a man 'at home' in his new house, accepting naturally his office of host. I do not think any of us could forget his concern for everyone's comfort. Apart from his brief experience of provincial rehearsals he of course realized that actors must keep different hours from other poeple. But as much as other people, if not more abundantly, actors must, he clearly felt, need to *be fed* . . . When did we have luncheon? Some of us had breakfasted at eight. By two p.m. he thought only our pathetically stout hearts prevented our fainting there on the stage from sheer inanition. When *did* we eat? Those like myself who played at night and had to make up, dress and be on the stage at eight o'clock — we hadn't lunched and we couldn't dine!

Before the more protracted last rehearsals ended Mr James had invoked his cook and his butler. Somewhere off-stage there used to appear a large hamper of delicacies to which with some ceremony Mr James would conduct us in two's or three's, as we happened also to be 'off'. He himself, sandwich in hand, would return to the fray with obvious relief and satisfaction, leaving us to make our more serious inroads. No other playwright in my tolerably wide experience ever thought of feeding his company.

Elizabeth Robins

On occasions . . . he would be not only accurate but concise. I met him at a dinner party once, shortly before the production of a play of his, and his hostess asked him if he did not find rehearsals a great strain. To which he replied: 'I have been sipping the — er — cup of Detachment.' No phrase could be a more perfect description of the state of mind to which most dramatists find themselves reduced at a certain stage of rehearsals.

F. Anstey

London Début

[*The American* was produced at the Opéra Comique in London on 26 September 1891.]

The American is a good, and even a remarkable, play . . . as was shewn by the interest with which it was followed by the house and the unstinted applause bestowed upon the performers and the author himself when the curtain fell.

The Times, 1891

Here is a man who writes stories with infinite art, who has studied the stage in England and in France, who has written penetrating essays on actors and acting; and yet when it comes to the construction of an actual play — the mere stage-carpentry which a stage-carpenter of the rank of Messrs. Buchanan and Sims would never bungle over — here is the man of letters as utterly out of his element as the stage-carpenters would be in their endeavour to write a piece of literature like, let us say, *Roderick Hudson*.

Arthur Symons in *The Academy, 1891*

The love scene in *The American* played by [Elizabeth Robins] with Edward Compton was so natural and so beautiful that it still lingers in my memory as the most perfect love scene I have ever witnessed on the stage.

C. C. H. Millar, 1937

My own suspense has been and still is great — though the voices of the air, rightly heard, seem to whisper *prosperity*. The papers have been on the whole quite awful — but the audiences are altogether different.

H. J. to E. Gosse, 2 October 1891

Honourable Death

[30 December] *The American* died an honourable death on the seventy-sixth night. It seemed, as far as the interest and enthusiasm of the audience went, a great success, but owing to a disastrous season for all theatres, and Compton being new and impecunious, the run was shorter than we hoped . . .

The whole episode was so shot through with the golden threads of comedy that we grew fat with laughter. The best moment was one afternoon when H. [? arrived] with the strangest amused, amazed, disgusted-with-himself expression, and said that he had just got a telegram from Compton telling him that the Prince of Wales was coming to the theatre that night, and wanting him to 'dress' a couple of boxes with 'smart people'. In the most pathetic voice H. exclaimed: 'Here I am, having put away my self-respecting papers, come out to do it! I'd do anything for the good Compton, but it will make me charitable to the end of my days.' . . .

Another fortunate accident was Harry's arriving at the theatre at the nick of time to hear the accomplished artist that acted the Marquis [Sydney Paxton] ask Compton, on his seventieth night of acting, 'why he was so anxious to give the letter to Madame de Cintré in the fourth act.' This is the sort of material H. has had to work over, and he has toiled like a galley-slave. He has been so manly, generous and unirritated by all the little petty incidents and exhibitions; so entirely occupied with the instructive side that one has had infinite satisfaction in him. He has had the most delightful relations with all the company, and he says the Comptons are of an inconceivable respectability; he has never even heard Compton say 'damn' at the most exasperating crisis!

Alice James, 1891

'My Real Form'

[After its honourable death in London *The American* remained in
Compton's provincial repertory for some time — the author having been
reluctantly prevailed upon to rewrite the fourth act with a conventional
'happy ending'.

Tenants and the unnamed 'admirable comedy' had been written before
the provincial production of *The American*, and in February 1891 a
fourth play, also unnamed, had been begun.]

Bear with me . . . so long as I am in the fever of dramatic production with which I am, very sanely and practically, trying to make
up for my late start and all the years during which I have *not*
dramatically produced, and, further, to get well ahead with the
'demand' which I — and others for me — judge (still very sanely
and sensibly) to be *certain* to be made upon me from the moment
I have a *London*, as distinguished from a provincial success . . .
Now that I have tasted blood, c'est une rage (of determination to
do, and triumph, on my part), for I feel at last as if I had found my
real form, which I am capable of carrying far, and for which the
little pale art of fiction, as I have practised it, has been, for me,
but a limited and restricted substitute . . . At any rate I am
working hard and constantly — and am just attacking my 4th!

H. J. to William James, 6 February 1891

MRS JASPER

[For the next two years James continued, as he wrote to R. L. Stevenson,
to 'hammer at the horrid little theatrical problem, with delays and inter-
missions'. Encouragement came from two quarters: from Augustin
Daly, the New York manager whose company, including Ada Rehan
and Arthur Bourchier, were regular visitors to London, and from
George Alexander the actor-manager of the St James's theatre. In the
summer of 1892 at Daly's suggestion James submitted a comedy, *Mrs
Jasper*; in the autumn, to meet Daly's criticisms, he 'materially
reconstructed and improved' it.]

The production of the play was postponed for a year with the
intention of putting it in rehearsal for Daly's new theatre in

London. As the time approached the solicitude of the manager led him to propose further revision, and the author wrote (6 November 1893):

I have given very earnest consideration to the text of my play, but with an utter failure to discover anything that can come out without injury. It was in the extremity of my effort at concision and rapidity during my writing of it as it now stands that I took out and kept out everything that was *not* intensely brief — and this effort seems to me to have left nothing behind to sacrifice — nothing that can be sacrificed without detriment to elementary clearness — to the rigid logic of the action and the successive definite steps of the story . . . Moreover, as it stands the thing appears to me to go — as if at least it *ought* to go — with remarkable brightness and quickness. If the public don't feel in it the *maximum* of that quality the public will — I can't help thinking — be a bigger ass than usual! If later, when we can talk of it — you are moved to *shew* me any definite place where anything can be, to your sense, spared, I shall of course be very happy to consider it . . . I shall keep myself wholly open to impressions at rehearsal and be only too eager to keep an eye on the text in the light of that test. I enclose a paper on which I have indited as many possible titles as I can think of — good, bad and indifferent . . .

The discussion of titles (to supersede *Mrs Jasper*) was thorough and the list enclosed by Mr James was of more than fifty names suggested by the leading points of the play. The result of all this care on the part of author and manager was disappointing. The piece was put in rehearsal and scenery purchased; but Augustin lost faith in *Mrs Jasper* and the attempt to bring it out was therefore given up. It will be found[1] in Mr James's collections of plays published in London in 1894.

                                                                J. F. Daly

'Ghastly!'

Only a word to say that the result (for your very sympathetic ear) of the ghastly — yes, it's the word! — two hours I have just brought to a close at Daly's is that I write to him tonight to

---

[1 With the title *Disengaged*.]

withdraw my piece. The 'rehearsal' left me in such a state of nervous exasperation that I judged it best — or rather I could only control myself and trust myself enough — to say simply to him after the last word was spoken: 'I shall take some hours to become perfectly clear to myself as to the reflections which this occasion — taken in connexion with your note of Saturday, causes me to make. And then I will write to you' — and then to walk out of the theatre.

H. J. to E. Robins, 6 December 1893

[Elizabeth Robins] has been a comfort to me ces-jours-ci on the occasion of a horrid désagrément — my withdrawing from Daly (provoked thereto by his calculated — or calculating — arts) the play he has had from me this last twelve month, and was (in my candid vision) to have produced a month hence. He is an abyss — but not an abyss of interest. Therefore basta.

H. J. to Mrs Hugh Bell, 6 December 1893

I wish I could give you some correspondingly good tidings of my own ascensory movement; but I had a fall — or rather took a jump — the other day (a month ago) of which the direction was not vulgarly — I mean theatrically and financially — upward . . . It was none the less for a while a lively disgust and disappointment — a waste of patient and ingenious labour and a sacrifice of coin much counted on. But à la guerre comme à la guerre. I mean to wage this war ferociously for one year more — 1894 — and then (unless the victory and the spoils have by that become more proportionate than hitherto to the humiliations and vulgarities and disgusts, all the dishonour and chronic insult incurred) to 'chuck' the whole intolerable experiment and return to more elevated and more independent courses . . . However, Alexander's preparations [of *Guy Domville*] are going on sedulously . . . He will produce me at no distant date, infallibly.

H. J. to William James, 29 December 1893

GUY DOMVILLE

The two men [H. J. and George Alexander] met. Henry James had three subjects in his mind: a three-act contemporary comedy, a three-act contemporary play, 'less purely a comedy but on a subject very beautiful to my sense', and *Guy Domville*, a play set in the eighteenth century. Unfortunately it was *Guy Domville* which was preferred by both men, and Henry James retired to Wellington Crescent, Ramsgate, to get on with the work. The script of the first act was sent, scenarios of the last two followed. Alexander was asked to remember that James was fully aware 'of the lacunae which real treatment of the subject must make good (and will); all the transitions it will smooth over, all the insufficiently explained things it will vivify, all the expression and colour, all the lucidity and atmosphere and superiority I shall undertake to make it supply' . . .

Henry James then took his courage in both hands to mention in advance — he seems in their conversation to have kept this little matter slyly up his sleeve — that 'his dénouement does not belong to the class of ending conventionally termed happy'. '*Mrs Tanqueray,*' he writes, 'seems to me to have performed the very valuable service of shewing that the poor dear old British public, in whose name such imbecilities are committed, can rise to a dénouement that isn't a mere daub of rose-colour.' Henry in fact was up on his toes.

A. E. W. Mason

Rehearsal

[In November 1893, a few days before the abortive rehearsal of *Mrs Jasper*, James was busying himself at the St James's theatre with the sets and costumes for *Guy Domville*. Five months later Alexander told the first-night audience of Henry Arthur Jones's *The Masqueraders* that he 'had ready, when it was wanted, a new play by Henry James', and more than another six months passed before *Domville* finally went into rehearsal. The cast included Alexander, H. V. Esmond, Marion Terry, Evelyn Millard and Irene Vanbrugh. W. G. Elliot played Lord Devenish.]

Well do I remember a good score off me at rehearsal by the author — who was too charming and kindly a man ever to have made it knowingly — when he came up to me and said in his curious, always fishing for the absolutely correct word way: 'Elliot, in your playing of this riotous — I mean "dissolute" — old — I should say "middle-aged" — peer, may I suggest — "hint" would be the better word — to you that you should endeavour — "try" — to make him as much of a gentleman as is feasible — "possible" — to you!'

W. G. Elliot

Before the Play

[*Guy Domville* opened at the St James's theatre on the evening of Saturday 5 January 1895.]

George Alexander was sanguine of success, and to do Henry James honour such a galaxy of artistic, literary and scientific celebrity gathered in the stalls of the St James's theatre as perhaps were never seen in a London playhouse before or since. Henry James was positively storm-ridden with emotion before the fatal night, and full of fantastic plans. I recall that one was that he should hide in the bar of a little public-house down an alley close to the theatre, whither I should slip forth at the end of the second act and report 'how it was going'.

Edmund Gosse

Don't after all, trouble to come to seek me on Saturday evening at the little nestling pub; for I have changed my policy. I recognize that the only way for me to arrive at 10 o'clock with any patience is to *do* something active or at least positive; so I have had the luminous idea of going to see some other play. I shall go and sit at the Garrick or the Haymarket till about 10.45 — or 11 — and then I will come into the theatre; at which moment you will be, I trust, in your enraptured stall. All thanks for the charitable intention I frustrate. The 2nd act isn't over till 10.15, or 10.30 even,

and it is to get *to* that period (at the pub. or at home) that would
be the devil.

H. J. to E. Gosse, 3 January 1895

On the night of the 5th, too nervous to do anything else, I had the
ingenious thought of going to some other theatre and seeing some
other play as a means of being coerced into quietness from 8 till
10.45. I went accordingly to the Haymarket, to a new piece by
[Oscar Wilde] . . . *An Ideal Husband*. I sat through it and saw it
played with every appearance (so far as the crowded house was
an appearance) of complete success, and *that* gave me the most
fearful apprehension. The thing seemed to me so helpless, so
crude, so bad, so clumsy, feeble and vulgar, that as I walked
away across St James's Square to learn my own fate, the prosperity of what I had seen seemed to me to constitute a dreadful
presumption of the shipwreck of *G. D.*, and I stopped in the
middle of the Square, paralysed by the terror of this probability —
afraid to go on and learn more.

H. J. to William James, 2 February 1895

First Night, Act I

I was one of the audience at the first night of his *Guy Domville* at
the St James's — a very terrible first night indeed. It was a
costume play; the period early Georgian; George Alexander
played the name-part and was extremely well supported, while
the stage sets designed by Edwin Abbey were charming. For a
time all seemed to be going well, the dialogue, being Henry
James's, was exquisitely phrased, and the house listened to it
attentively. But before the first act was over it was clear that the
play was not gripping the audience; the coughs which are so
infallible a sign of it grew more and more frequent. However, the
house was full of his friends and admirers, and the applause at the
end of the act was loud enough, though it came chiefly from the
stalls and dress circle.

F. Anstey

Act II

With the next act came a change. The author had done a dangerous
thing in dropping most of the first-act characters and introducing a
new set in whom little interest was taken. The excellence of the
opening was now a drawback, the audience wanted more of it;
they longed to follow the fortunes of Marion Terry and sulkily
refused to be interested in the doings of Miss Millard.

An elderly actress [Mrs Edward Saker] entered in a costume
which struck them as grotesque. As a fact the dress was a particularly fine one, but it wanted wearing; the huge hoop and great
black hat[1] perched upon a little frilled under-cap should have been
carried by one filled with the pride of them and the consciousness
of their beauty. But at the unexpected laughter the actress took
fright, she became timid, apologetic, she tried to efface herself.
Now the spectacle of a stately dame whose balloon-like skirts half
filled the stage and whose plumes smote the heavens trying to
efface herself was genuinely ludicrous, and the laugh became a
roar. After this the audience got out of hand; they grew silly and
cruel and ready to jeer at everything.

W. Graham Robertson

Act III

The last act, with its lovely White Parlour and the longed-for
return of Marion Terry, almost pulled things together again, but
by this time the hero's continual vacillations between his lady-
loves had struck the demoralized house as comic, and when he
changed his mind for the last time the irreverent let themselves go.

W. Graham Robertson

Alexander at the close had an incredibly awkward exit. He had
to stand at a door in the middle of the stage, say slowly, 'Be
keynd to Her . . . *Be* keynd to Her' and depart. By nature

[1] '. . . like a gigantic fur muff. It had, I believe, been copied from a contemporary
print and was strictly of the period.' — *F. Anstey*.

Alexander had a long face, but at that moment, with audible defeat before him, he seemed the longest and dismallest face, all face, that I have ever seen. The slowly closing door reduced him to a strip, to a line, of perpendicular gloom. The uproar burst like a thunderstorm as the door closed and the stalls responded with feeble applause. Then the tumult was mysteriously allayed. There were some minutes of uneasy apprehension. 'Author,' cried voices. 'Au-thor!' The stalls, not understanding, redoubled their clapping.

H. G. Wells

Curtain

As the curtain was falling on the last act Henry James entered the theatre by the stage door. He was informed that all had gone well. No one told him that a rough in the gallery had shouted at the end — when George Alexander had said, 'I'm the *last*, my lord, of the Domvilles' — 'It's a damned good thing you are!'

Leon Edel[1]

Disaster was too much for Alexander that night. A spasm of hate for the writer of those fatal lines must surely have seized him. With incredible cruelty he led the doomed James, still not understanding clearly how things were with him, to the middle of the stage, and there the pit and gallery had him. James bowed; he knew it was the proper thing to bow. Perhaps he had selected a few words to say, but if so they went unsaid. I have never heard any sound more devastating than the crescendo of booing that ensued. The gentle applause of the stalls was altogether overwhelmed. For a moment or so James faced the storm, his round face white, his mouth opening and shutting, and then Alexander,

---

[1] From information supplied by Miss Irene Vanbrugh and a theatre attendant. A less reliable version of this incident (the name of the play is given as *Roderick Hudson*) appears in Walter Sichel's *Sands of Time*.

I hope in a contrite mood, snatched him back into the wings.[1]

H. G. Wells

The Critics

Since *Beau Austin* [by W. E. Henley and R. L. Stevenson] we have seen nothing on the English stage so charming as the first act of *Guy Domville*. The motives are delicately interwoven, yet remain clear and convincing; the scenes are ordered with a master hand; and the writing is graceful without mannerism.

W. Archer in *The World, 1895*

We want more Henry Jameses to write for the stage, not less of them . . . The first act of *Guy Domville* is one of the most beautiful human documents that has been committed to the care of the stage for some time. The man who can write that first act will one day write a play that will live.

C. Scott in the *Daily Telegraph, 1895*

[*Guy Domville* was] listened to with a degree of patience which a more experienced dramatist than Mr James could not have hoped for . . . It is vain to insist upon the literary merits of an

[1] On 9 January 1895 the *Westminster Gazette* wrote that there had been on the first night 'a cabal against the piece' and that the hissing in the gallery and upper boxes had begun at a concerted signal. 'Moreover we have heard upon really good authority that upon Saturday before the performance Mr Alexander received a telegram, "With hearty wishes for a complete failure".' James referred to this telegram (handed in at the Sloane Street post office by two ladies) in a letter to Elizabeth Robins. Correspondents of the *Westminster* next day scouted the possibility of a cabal and the rumour gradually died.

Twenty-five years later Gosse revived the rumour which he said, without adducing evidence, had been confirmed; and a writer in the *Literary Digest* in 1920 alleged on the authority of unnamed documents that the cabal was formed by the friends of an actress who had been engaged for an important part but had been superseded during the rehearsals. Ten years later again F. M. Hueffer wrote that the audience was angry with Alexander because the first night of *Guy Domville* was also the first night on which a charge was made for theatre programmes. The problem is perhaps now insoluble.

unsuccessful play or to question the popular verdict that has condemned it. Like every author who ventures into the dramatic arena, Mr Henry James aims at pleasing the public, and missing his mark, no matter from what cause — over-elaboration, mistaken choice of subject, insincerity of treatment, or superfine writing — he fails. All these faults and more *Guy Domville* possesses in a marked degree. In every scene, in almost every line, it tells of painful and misdirected effort.

The Times, 1895

Guy Domville, that beautiful, harshly treated play . . .

The Times, 1930

The truth about Mr James's play is no worse than that it is out of fashion . . . Is it good sense to accuse Mr Henry James of a want of grip of the realities of life because he gives us a hero who sacrifices his love to a strong and noble vocation for the Church? And yet when some unmannerly playgoer, untouched by either love or religion, chooses to send a derisive howl from the gallery at such a situation, we are to sorrowfully admit, if you please, that Mr James is no dramatist, on the general ground that 'the drama's laws the drama's patrons give'. Pray which of its patrons? — the cultivated majority who, like myself and all the ablest of my colleagues, applauded Mr James on Saturday, or the handful of rowdies who brawled at him? It is the business of the dramatic critic to educate these dunces, not to echo them.

Admitting, then, that Mr James's dramatic authorship is valid, and that his plays are *du théâtre* when the right people are in the theatre, what are the qualities and faults of *Guy Domville*? First among the qualities, a rare charm of speech. Line after line comes with such a delicate turn and fall that I unhesitatingly challenge any of our popular dramatists to write a scene in verse with half the beauty of Mr James's prose . . . Second, *Guy Domville* is a story, and not a mere situation hung out on a gallows of plot. And it is a story of fine sentiment and delicate manners, with an

entirely worthy and touching ending . . . It will be a deplorable
misfortune if *Guy Domville* does not hold the stage long enough
to justify Mr Alexander's enterprise in producing it.

G. B. Shaw in the *Saturday Review, 1895*

The Reaction

Early next morning I called at 34 De Vere Gardens, hardly daring
to press the bell for fear of the worst of news, so shattered with
excitement had the playwright been on the previous evening. I
was astonished to find him perfectly calm; he had slept well and
was breakfasting with appetite. The theatrical bubble in which he
had lived a tormented existence for five years was wholly and
finally broken, and he returned, even in that earliest conversation, to the discussion of the work which he had so long and so
sadly neglected, the art of direct prose narrative. And now a
remarkable thing happened. The discipline of toiling for the
caprices of the theatre had amounted, for so redundant an imaginative writer, to the putting on of a mental strait-jacket . . . I
recall his saying to me, after the fiasco of *Guy Domville*, 'At all
events I have escaped for ever from the foul fiend Excision!'

Edmund Gosse

[The immediate reaction of the playwright to the failure of his most
ambitious venture may be seen also in certain of the *Letters*, too long to
be quoted here. He inveighed against the 'abysmal vulgarity and
brutality of the theatre and its regular public', comforted himself with an
abundance of private praise, described himself as 'a Rock', spoke of
publishing *Domville* ('it's altogether the best thing I've done' — though
he never did publish it) and before the run was over was writing to
Howells of his intention of returning to prose fiction.

Domville was taken off on 5 February, 'whisked away to make room
for the triumphant Oscar'. James had already decided to publish four of
his rejected plays. Two, *Tenants* and *Disengaged*, had appeared in 1894;
to the other two, *The Album* and *The Reprobate*, 1895, he prefixed an
introduction in which he summed up the lesson he had learnt and which
may be regarded as closing his first period as a dramatist.]

The Last Word

As long as seventeen years after the failure of . . . *Guy Domville*
. . . he acknowledged to me that there was a certain justice in the
adverse verdict originally pronounced upon that work. 'Instead
of making the dramatic interest my sole or even my chief consideration,' he said, 'I aimed at a supreme technical victory in
observing a unity for unity's sake. Consequently it was too
compressed; and I now have dreams of re-writing it in four acts
instead of the original three.'

H. M. Walbrook

H. J. AS PLAYGOER

[If James's disappointment at the collapse of his theatrical schemes was
bitter his revulsion against the theatre was less complete than many of
his biographers and critics have represented. Within a few months of the
failure of *Guy Domville* he was reading to a friend a one-act comedy
which he had written for Ellen Terry, was helping to revise a translation
of Echegaray's *Mariana* and was attending every London production of
importance, often to write of it in *Harper's Weekly*.]

The Startled Stalls

. . . an invitation . . . to dine with him 'very slightly' before the
play, on 'chicken and fixings'; or '. . . I will look out for you this
evening at the theatre door — to "arm" you in — up to 8 o'clock
when I will, failing your visibility, seek the security of the box.'

I see him again standing there, anxious, solicitous, and then
being gaily claimed, seeking in haste 'the security of the box.' I see
him listening warily to the play, or in an entr'acte to his
companion, with that look all of us, not least his devoted friends,
came to know — the look of silent inward laughter; a laughter
never with safety to be interpreted as with, but *at* something or
somebody, probably the one nearest . . .

It is forgivable, I hope, to admit that going with Mr James to
English plays sometimes demanded what our Florida cook would

call 'de bol' courage'. One never grew wholly acclimatized to the nipping airs that now and then would blow about the startled stalls. Mr James's all too audible remarks, conveyed in terms always 'chosen', often singularly picturesque, sometimes diabolic — as though he revelled in mercilessness — would send cold shivers down his companion's spine. She could tell without looking that the lucky people on each side, or immediately in front or behind — whether they, 'poor dears', were enjoying the play or not — very certainly were enjoying Mr James. As for me, at such times I could only sit tingling under a series of shocks. To remonstrate however discreetly made things worse. From a denunciation so 'lively' that it was deadly the critic would fall to a still more scathing pity, in which I would find myself involved.

It was a different matter when the play was French or Italian, and not always, I used to think, because it was actually so much better. The alien tongue, the nature as well as the art of the Latin, appealed strongly to Henry James; they found his guard down. He could 'give' himself to the foreign actor as I never saw him so much as begin to do in the case of anyone speaking English. I remember a moment between the acts of *Chamillac* when in his eager explanation and enforcement I realized with a jolt of incredulity that never once in the entire repertory had the smallest hole been picked in Coquelin. Mr James was actually content merely to 'follow' and enjoy!!

Yet not entirely content until he had done all in his power to carry his guest along with him. It was as though he couldn't, in courtesy, leave her so far behind if it could be helped. In that way it came about, out of his desire to enable me to distinguish, that I learned how little of Coquelin's art, of his temperamental responsiveness, his wit, his subtlety, his triumphant technique were wasted on Henry James.

Elizabeth Robins

Knoblock and Shaw

When I was in London he generally joined me there for a day or two, especially if any theatrical event were impending; and I remember going one evening with him to see Mr Knoblock's Arabian Nights' fantasy *Kismet*, then an innovation in stage-setting and lighting. We were enchanted with this lovely evocation of the bazaars to which all London was thronging . . . Another evening we went to *Androcles and the Lion*, and I think James laughed as much as I did at that enormous fooling, though doubtless with more self-restraint. In reality he was a much better theatre-goer than I, for the material limitations of the stage and its violent fore-shortenings, which always contract my vision and cut rudely into my dream, seemed to stimulate his imagination, however much he found to criticize in a given play or its acting.

Edith Wharton

'Imbecile Rot!'

I will frankly confess that I hated to go with him to the theatre. In the years before the War I went many times, and always there was the same catastrophe. We sat in the front or second row of the stalls, James very noticeable in his smartness, stockiness, alertness, and carrying with him a gold-headed cane. Very soon the cane would begin to tap the floor, then, as the play proceeded, the taps would become more furious. At the end of the first act he would inquire my opinions. I learnt very soon to be cautious, but hedge as I might I was always too kindly. At the end of the second act it was likely as not that he would rise, pronounce only too audibly 'Rot! Imbecile rot!' and trot furiously from the theatre, I meekly following.

Hugh Walpole

Dining with us one night he said he'd like to go to a theatre: I asked him, would he like to see the play that at the moment was the most popular? He said he would. I warned him that it possessed no special literary merit, but was just a pleasant, well-made, quasi-sentimental comedy. He would be glad to see it, he said, to be shewn what kind of things went down with the people. So I got a box and we went, Henry James, my wife and I.

The first act was gay and bright; we said nothing when the curtain fell, but talked of other things. The second act was the best, and really very ingenious and amusing; there was a constant ripple of laughter through the house, a sense of delighted enjoyment. Henry James gave no sign, and watch him as I might I could not discern a smile. The curtain fell; it had to be raised half-a-dozen times, so great was the applause, the enthusiasm. I turned to him: 'Well, Mr James,' I said, 'what do you think of it?' 'My dear Alfred,' came the unhesitating reply, 'I think it nauseating.'

Alfred Sutro

In his whimsical way he even attributed the very trying illness which laid him low at Rye in the autumn and winter of 1912 to an evening spent at a West End theatre!

H. M. Walbrook

THE SECOND PERIOD

[After Ellen Terry had kept the one-act play, *Mrs Gracedew*, for two years without showing any anxiety to make use of it — it was written to take one hour and she wanted half-an-hour taken out of it — James wrote it into a long-short story, 'Covering End.' The publication of the story in 1898 in *The Two Magics* (the other being 'The Turn of the Screw') stimulated George Alexander to ask for the play, but nothing came of this. William Archer, considering the play for the New Century theatre, saw it as 'a gem with a single flaw' but nothing came of this either. Forbes Robertson also asked to see it in 1899, but seven or eight years seem to have elapsed before he suggested that James should expand it into a three-act comedy. James did so in the autumn of 1907 and when *The High Bid*, as it was now called, proved too short to fill an evening bill he threw in for good measure a curtain-raiser, *The Saloon*, which he vamped up from an old short story, *Owen Wingrave*, within a fortnight. The theatrical fever was on him once more.

The course of this new fever, the rises and falls of temperature with alternating hopes and disappointments, need not be followed here: much of it appears in the *Letters* and little new — beyond James's petulant description of Forbes Robertson as '*the* typical mountebank' — has been published since Leon Edel's essay on *Les Années dramatiques*, 1931. But to round off the story, and to show how the Master persisted with 'the horrid little theatrical problem' to the end, a list may be given of the completed plays of the second dramatic period.

——*The High Bid* was unsuccessfully produced by Forbes Robertson in Edinburgh on 26 March 1908 and the following week at Glasgow. The London production was limited to five matinées at His Majesty's theatre in February 1909.

——*The Saloon* was successfully produced by Gertrude Kingston at the Little theatre in January-February 1911.

——*The Other House*, first written as a play in the mid-nineties, was converted into a novel, published in 1896. It was rewritten as a play again in 1909, read to Harley Granville-Barker with a view to inclusion in Charles Frohman's repertory at the Duke of York's theatre, but rejected.

——*The Outcry* was written in 1909-10, announced in the press as being added to the Duke of York's repertory, and the cast (including John Hare, who had failed to put on *Tenants* some twenty years earlier) selected; but Frohman's repertory venture came to an end before it went into rehearsal. James rewrote *The Outcry* as a novel, published in 1911: the play was ultimately produced by the Stage Society in 1917, after his death.

Finally in 1913 James wrote a monologue for Miss Ruth Draper, the American *diseuse*. Though he hoped it would prove a 'really practical, *doable* little affair' it was never performed: it may be read in the *London Mercury* for September 1922.]

Persian Carpet

H. J. was greatly interested in my work and wrote the sketch just on the chance I might do it (as my own!). He pleaded for anonymity. I never felt I could do it — and certainly not *as my own* — for it bore his peculiar stamp. I think he was disappointed, but I never learned it or tried it on anyone.

I used to talk to him about my work and ask his counsel as to

The Legend of the Master

whether I should concentrate on writing or acting as a career, and going definitely on the stage in plays. He replied: 'My dear child . . . you . . . have woven . . . your own . . . very beautiful . . . little Persian carpet . . . Stand on it!'

Ruth Draper

OF PERSONS

MAINLY WRITERS

[These are only conversational fragments. Similar dicta about the same and other writers may be found scattered in James's letters, and formal appreciations of many of them in his published critical works.]

George Sand

We talked . . . of George Sand, of whom he said: 'She was a man: a woman can transform herself into a man, but never into a gentleman!'

John Bailey, 1914

In the intervals between dining out he liked a dash in the motor; and among other jolly expeditions I remember a visit to Nohant, when he saw for the first time George Sand's house. I had been there before, and knew how to ingratiate myself with the tall impressive guardian of the shrine, a handsome *Berrichonne* who could remember, as a very little girl, helping 'Madame' to dress Maurice's marionettes, which still dangled wistfully from their hooks in the little theatre below stairs . . .

He lingered delightedly over the puppet theatre with Maurice's grimacing dolls, and the gay costumes stitched by his mother; then we wandered out into the garden, and looking up at the plain old house tried to guess behind which windows the various famous visitors had slept. James stood there a long time, gazing and brooding beneath the row of closed shutters. 'And in which of those rooms, I wonder, did George herself sleep?' I heard him suddenly mutter. 'Though in which, indeed' — with a twinkle —

'in which indeed, my dear, did she *not*?'

Edith Wharton

Tennyson

Old Henry James, with his odd slowness, has given me some delightful talks; of which I only note his feelings of the mediocrity and narrowness of Tennyson — the one thing in which he vexed me — and I think he is all wrong, though of course there is a bourgeois limited side of Tennyson.

John Bailey, 1908

George Eliot

Sometimes, in a friendly spirit, people would bait him. Once someone, to do so, asked him what must have been the feelings of Mr Cross,[1] the husband of George Eliot, on hearing that his wife had died. James considered it intensely, and answered slowly: 'Agony . . . Dismay . . . Amazement . . . Fear . . . ' Then suddenly his face lighted. He threw up his hands and almost shouted: '*Relief!*'

Stephen Spender

Turgenev

Henry James once said to me. . . 'Ah, he was the real . . . but a thousand times the only — the only real, beautiful genius!' He added: 'One qualifies it with "Russian" for immediateness of

---

[1] Mr Spender printed 'Lewes' for 'Cross'. Mr Spender tells me that he had the anecdote from Lady Ottoline Morrell. The uncertainty of oral tradition is well illustrated by a comparison of this version with that given by Sir Edward Marsh: '. . . his pensive answer to someone who asked what he supposed George Eliot's husband, J. W. Cross, to have felt when she died: "Regret . . . remorse . . . RELIEF".' Sir Edward Marsh tells me that he had the story from Gosse, and adds: 'I've never been quite sure about the second word, as I don't see why he should have felt Remorse — but Regret and Relief are certainly authentic, and I can't think of any other word beginning with "Re-" that would fit.'

identification by the unknowing. But for you, for me, for us . . .
for all of us who are ever so little in as you might say the know of
literary values, he must always be just that, *tout court* . . . the
beautiful, beautiful genius.'

                                                                F. M. Hueffer

Whitman

We talked long that night of *Leaves of Grass*, tossing back and
forth to each other treasure after treasure; but finally James, in
one of his sudden humorous drops from the heights, flung up his
hands and cried out with the old stammer and twinkle: 'Oh, yes, a
great genius; undoubtedly a very great genius! Only one cannot
help deploring his too extensive acquaintance with the foreign
languages.'

                                                                Edith Wharton

Du Maurier

Henry James, I heard from du Maurier, came up to New Grove
House after *Trilby* had become the talk of the town, and invited
him to come for a walk. 'Let us,' said Henry James, 'find a seat and
sit down and endeavour — if it is in any way possible to arrive at
a solution — to discover some reason for such a phenomenon as
the success of *Trilby*.'

                                                                F. Anstey

Walter Pater . . .

He was telling that in a certain chapter [of *Marius the Epicurean*]
towards the end of the second volume Pater took Christianity
under his personal wing, diminishing thereby the aesthetic value
of his work and unnecessarily, for in the next chapter he allows us
to see the power that Christian ceremonial exercises on Marius.
His words are — May I have the book, Miss Robinson? Mary
returned with the book and James read: What has been on the

whole the method of the Church as a power of sweetness and patience in dealing with matters like Pagan art was already manifest; it has the character of the divine moderation of Christ Himself. Now no human or divine being, James said, laying the book aside, was ever less moderate than Christ Himself, and it is hard for me to believe that Pater read the Gospels so carelessly that the outbursts escaped his notice. But, my dear Mr Henry James, Pater wishes to present Jesus in two aspects. It seems to me, Miss Robinson, the words divine moderation present Him in one. Pater may hint darkly that there is another side, but he keeps that other side out of sight, but if we say any more we shall be provoked into a morass of Biblical disputation; so I will say that when Miss Vernon Lee spoke as she did just now of Renan, I understood her to mean that Pater adopts a tone as conciliatory as Renan. I have praised Pagan civilization, but you shall see in a moment how nicely I can speak about Christian. But would you not have had him speak nicely about Christian civilization, Mr James? interposed Mabel Robinson.

George Moore

. . . and Miss Pater

I once asked him to pay a call on the sole surviving sister of Walter Pater. The poor lady lived much alone. I fear that the visit was not a success . . . Hester Pater glared at him and told him that she hated 'horrid' ghost stories about children. This turn of the screw became so painful that we soon rose to go. On the doorstep of the tiny house, whence he was perfectly audible from within, James discriminated long and loud in this manner: 'Pater? *Walter* Pater? Well, yes. Yes, well enough — after a fashion; that fashion being of a kind somehow prone — I might say calculated — to bring forth, to be conducive to, *legend*. Part of the legend survives in there; the old lady, I mean, survives. She looks *cross*. I suspect she *is* cross. May crossness explain her solitude?' I believe these two survivors had no second meeting.

Richard Jennings

Meredith

He spoke of George Meredith in terms of generous admiration — of the heroism of his life, his struggle against poverty and adversity, the high and gallant spirit with which he sat and watched bodily decrepitude creep on, with never a syllable of complaint. But he had been re-reading the Italian novels and was astonished to find in how many ways they managed to be incredibly bad . . . And what are we to make of the England [Meredith] draws? An England of fabulous 'great' people, of coaching, prize-fighting and yachting, flavoured with the regency yet incapable of precise location in space and time.

S. P. Waterlow, 1907

I think that only one contributor to my first two numbers did not tell me that the [*English*] *Review* was ruined by the inclusion of all the other contributors. James said: 'Poor old Meredith, he writes these mysterious nonsenses and heaven alone knows what they all mean.' — Meredith had contributed merely a very short account of his dislike for Rossetti's breakfast manners. It was as comprehensible as a seedsman's catalogue.

Meredith said, on looking at James's 'Jolly Corner,' which led off the prose of the *Review*: 'Poor old James, he sets down on paper these mysterious rumblings in his bowels — but who could be expected to understand them?'

F. M. Hueffer

Dominating the hearth, and all of us [at Howard Sturgis's house], Henry James stands, or heavily pads about the room, listening, muttering, groaning disapproval, or chuckling assent to the paradoxes of the other tea-drinkers. And then, when tea is over and the tray has disappeared, he stops his prowling to lean against the mantelpiece and plunge into reminiscences of the Paris or London of his youth, or into some slowly elaborated literary disquisition, perhaps on the art of fiction or the theatre, on Balzac, on Tolstoy, or better still on one of his own contemporaries. I remember especially one afternoon when the question: 'And Meredith — ?' suddenly freed a 'full-length' of that master which, I imagine, still hangs in the mental picture-galleries of all who heard him.

It began, mildly enough, with a discussion of Meredith's importance as a novelist, in which I think Howard was his principal champion. James, deep-sunk in an armchair and in silence, sat listening and weighing our views, till he suddenly pounced on my avowal that, much as I admired some of the novels, I had never been able to find out what any of them, except *The Egoist* and *Harry Richmond*, were about. I tried to temper this by adding that in many passages, and especially the descriptive ones, the author's style rose to a height of poetic imagery which — but here James broke in with the cry that I had put my finger on the central weakness of Meredith's art, its unconscious insincerity. Words — words — poetic imagery, metaphors, epigrams, descriptive passages! How much did any of them weigh in the baggage of the authentic novelist? (By this time he was on his feet, swaying agitatedly to and fro before the fire.) Meredith, he continued, was a sentimental rhetorician, whose natural indolence or congenital insufficiency, or both, made him, in life as in his art, shirk every climax, dodge around it, and veil its absence in a fog of eloquence. Of course, he pursued, neither I nor any other reader could make out what Meredith's tales were about; and not only what they were about, but even in what country and what century they were situated, all these prosaic details being hopelessly befogged by the famous poetic imagery. He himself, James said, when he read Meredith, was always at a loss to know where he was, or what causes had led to which events, or even to discover by what form of conveyance the elusive characters he was struggling to identify moved from one point of the globe to another (except, Howard interpolated, that the heroines always did so on horseback); till at last the practical exigencies of the subject forced the author to provide some specific means of transport, and suddenly, through the fog of his verbiage, the reader caught the far-off tinkle of a bell that (here there was a dramatic pause of suspense) — that turned out to be that of a mere vulgar hansom-cab: 'Into which,' James concluded with his wicked twinkle, 'I always manage to leap before the hero, and drive straight out of the story.'

Such *boutades* implied no lack of appreciation of Meredith the poet, still less of regard for the man. James liked and admired Meredith, and esteemed him greatly for the courage and dignity with which he endured the trial of his long illness; but, when the sacred question of the craft was touched upon, all personal sympathies seemed irrelevant, and our friend pronounced his judgments without regard to them.[1]

Edith Wharton

Meredith and Hardy

Dr Garnett . . . told us the delicious saying of Henry James, describing Meredith and Hardy — Meredith the Obscure and the Amazing Hardy.

Michael Field, 1897

Hardy's Mother and First Wife

'The pathetic couple,' said Henry James, 'is devoted to *Genius Worship*. Were Heaven to inflict a wife on me, how content I should be if she did not despise the prerogatives of her sex and her beauty in her envy of the poor small talents of which the man as artist brags.'

J.-E. Blanche

[1] Cf. James's view of *Lord Ormont* in his letter to Edmund Gosse, 22 August 1894. That letter, written in Switzerland, appears to have been canvassed among Gosse's party, for a fortnight later James wrote to Arthur Benson: 'It makes me wince that my profanity about Meredith was repercussed among the mountain-tops. Please forget it, or don't impart it — as mine — to the Etonian mind. I hope that mind, by the way, is as different as may be from the boy-soul and the boy-talk G. Meredith sometimes, too often, paints — as in *Harry Richmond*, e.g. — though he has had some felicities with these things elsewhere.' (*Letters to A. C. Benson*, etc., 3.)

For James's later estimate of Meredith as a man, as well as a writer, see his letter to Gosse, 10–15 October 1912. It is interesting to note that Hardy once after reading something of James's wrote: 'It is remarkable that a writer who has no grain of poetry or humour or spontaneity in his productions can yet be a good novelist. Meredith has some poetry, and yet I can read James when I cannot look at Meredith.'

Zola

I was walking back with Henry James very late one night from Putney to Piccadilly . . . I had said good words of Zola, and had declared that the novelist was a very great writer. Then it came. Henry James, who truth to say I had always looked upon as a man of a mild temperament, one not given to letting his parts of speech get the better of him under any provocation whatsoever, vouchsafed to me his ideas on Zola, and that unholy Frenchman's degradation of literature, with a power of expression that left nothing to the imagination in respect either of directness or force. He stood in the middle of the road to do it: he could not spare breath for perambulation while the paroxysm lasted.

H. M. Hyndman

Henry James often spoke to me of Racine's princes and princesses, saying that these are singularly difficult to consider as human beings, to accept as individuals in their classical majesty, but that they are nevertheless more interesting to examine than the creatures drawn by realists such as Zola . . . He expressed his contempt for, and horror of, Zola's vulgarity.

J.-E. Blanche

Gissing

[James met George Gissing only once, in 1901. The first of the following extracts was written in Rye on the day of Gissing's death in Italy.]

Poor Gissing . . . struck me then as quite particularly marked out for what is called in his and my profession an unhappy ending.

H. J. to S. Colvin, 1903

How surprising that with so much humming and hawing, such deliberation in the choice of the right adjective, the portraits of persons that he builds up in talk should be so solid and vivid! Thus he described the only occasion on which he had seen

Gissing. The impression made by Gissing was a peculiarly painful one. Nature had been unkind to him. The front face was not bad; he had a fine forehead and clustering hair. But when he turned his head you saw one side of the face disfigured by a great expanse of purple scar, and mouth and chin were uncomely and feeble. Altogether an extraordinarily ungainly, common, ill-shaped figure; almost knock-kneed, bearing the unmistakable stamp of Wakefield, his birthplace. And how queer that such a being should speak French so well — with a precise affectation that made it almost *too* well!

S. P. Waterlow, 1907

Wilde

[Oscar Wilde was in Washington on his American lecture tour.]

We are urged to meet Oscar Wilde . . . Henry James went to call on him yesterday and says he is a 'fatuous cad'.

Mrs Henry Adams, 1882

Shaw

[In December 1907 Bernard Shaw contributed to *Everybody's Magazine*, under the title 'A Nation of Villagers', an article which his biographer describes as 'even for Shaw . . . of an exceptionally vitriolic character'.]

One day, meeting the late Henry James in London, I casually asked his opinion of Shaw's latest tirade against the United States. With that curious, dubitative, halting manner — as if he were vainly seeking the most just, but most elusive word: 'It is — er — oh — you see — er — quite a detail; but,' and here his eyes flashed fire, 'this unspeakable Irishman has never even visited the United States.'

Archibald Henderson

Ellen Terry

H. J. was complaining to us that Ellen Terry had asked him to write a play for her, and now that he had done so, and read it to her, had refused it. My wife, desiring to placate, asked: 'Perhaps she did not think the part suited to her?' H. J. turned upon us both, and with resonance and uplifting voice replied: 'Think? *Think?* How should the poor toothless, chattering hag THINK?' The sudden outpouring of improvised epithets had a most extraordinary effect. A crescendo on 'toothless' and then on 'chattering' and then on 'hag' — and 'think' delivered with the trumpet of an elephant.

Edmund Gosse

Anne Thackeray Ritchie

Henry James once told me that he thought she had 'every possible good quality except common sense'.

A. M. Brookfield

Two Women Novelists

The conversation turned on the novels of Thomas Hardy, and I expressed my feelings of many years before when I read *Tess* for the first time. The events and persons in that story seemed so real to me, and the catastrophe so overwhelming, that for days after I had finished it I could not shake off my depression. Miss Sinclair said that the same sense of reality impressed her in reading the novels of Mrs Humphry Ward. This appalled Henry James, who said, '*May Sinclair, May Sinclair*, such a remark may do credit to your heart, but where does it leave your head?'

W. L. Phelps

Santayana

'. . . Will you come to luncheon to meet him?'

'COME!' Henry James cried, raising his hands to Heaven. 'I would walk across London with bare feet on the snow to meet George Santayana.'

Logan Pearsall Smith

Lawrence

When he published his *Notes on Novelists* one of our friends, who had been greatly struck by Lawrence's *Sons and Lovers*, reproached James for having dealt so summarily with a new novelist who was beginning to attract the attention of intelligent readers. James's reply was evasive and unsatisfactory, and at last his interlocutor exclaimed: 'Come, now! Have you ever read any of Lawrence's novels — really read them?' James's most mischievous smile crept down from his eyes to his lips. 'I — I have trifled with the exordia,' he murmured.

Edith Wharton

Howells and James

He spoke of Howells with sincere love and appreciation. 'He is an artist — always — but he has written too much, and so have I.'

Hamlin Garland

Daudet on the Master

Henry James's voice dropped to a conversational level.

'I am now going to tell you a story,' he said. 'It's a story I have never told before, and shall never tell again; a story that in decency I never ought to tell. But now I shall indecently tell it!

'Some years ago my friend Alphonse Daudet was in London; he often came to see me and we met at dinners and luncheons. On the last of these occasions when he came to say farewell, "My dear friend," he remarked, "I have been observing you carefully for some months; I have met almost all your friends and acquaintances; *et je vois que vous demeurez parmi des gens moins fins que vous.*" That was what he said when he left England for Paris.'

Logan Pearsall Smith

PAINTERS

In view of the facts, the remark in *Truth* is very droll about the introduction that H. wrote for the catalogue of Alfred Parsons's exhibition of pictures — to the effect that, being a distinguished member of the Savile Club, 'Mr H. J. naturally writes a laudation of his friend Mr Parsons's pictures,' etc. — the truth being that H. loves not the Savile Club and goes there about once a year, and Mr. Parsons isn't a member at all.

H. said one day that Burne-Jones, Sargent and Alfred Parsons are the most complete artists he knows in their point of view, and in their natures the best of men.

Alice James, 1891

Holman Hunt

He gave me a depressing account of Holman Hunt's conversation, which he likened to a trickle of tepid water from a tap one is unable to turn off. 'There must be some way,' he said, 'one could do *so*, or *so*, or *so*' (imitating the gesture of turning a tap this way and that), 'but no, nothing will stop it, on it goes. Once I had occasion to visit an obscure street in Chelsea, and after trying for some time to find it, in an evil hour' (here his voice became sinister) 'I met Holman Hunt, who professed knowledge of it and offered to guide me. And for two mortal hours we wandered through the byways of Chelsea, while he talked on and on and on. He chose the not unattractive subject of Ruskin's marriage; but even that topic, which might in other hands have been alluring, proved in his not otherwise than DULL.'

Edward Marsh

Post-Impressionists

Among the daily press of unknown people there would appear now and then an old friend — Arnold Bennett for instance, or Henry James. Them [Fry] would take down to the basement where, among the packing cases and the brown paper, tea would be provided. Seated on a little hard chair Henry James would express 'in convoluted sentences the disturbed hesitations which Matisse and Picasso aroused in him, and Roger Fry, exquisitely, with something of the old-world courtesy which James carried about with him', would do his best to convey to the great novelist what he meant by saying that Cézanne and Flaubert were, in a manner of speaking, after the same thing.

Virginia Woolf

WOMEN

Friendships

James, I think, found his best friends among women. They liked him for various reasons. He had fame, and they liked him for that. Then there are women who particularly value the friendship of a clever and distinguished man because it is pleasing to their vanity. Some friendships of his with women I knew, I think, had this foundation. Women liked him also for his good looks and charming manners and his innate refinement. They liked him especially for his sympathetic and delicate discernment of their own nice qualities.

He seemed to look at women rather as women look at them. Women look at women as persons; men look at them as women. The quality of sex in women, which is their first and chief attraction to most men, was not their chief attraction to James.

E. S. Nadal

Once or twice I went a round of calls with him. I remember being struck on these occasions by how much woman there seemed to be in him; at least it was thus I explained the concentration of his sympathy upon social worries (the wrong people meeting each other, etc., etc.), or small misfortunes such as missing a train, and also the length of time he was able to expatiate upon them with interest. It struck me that women ran on in talk with him with a more unguarded volubility than they do with most men, as though they were sure of his complete understanding.

Desmond MacCarthy

Marriage

Of all the men I ever knew he was the man whom I could least imagine with a wife. When he would be recommending matrimony to me and I would say, 'Why don't you?' he would reply with quiet conviction: 'I am not a marrying man.'

He may have been sorry for this later . . . An American lady, the mother of children, met him in London in company with several persons who like himself were childless; she told me that he said to her: 'You are the only one of us who has accomplished what is after all the most important and the most desirable thing in life.'

E. S. Nadal

A Proposal?

Lunched with Mrs Procter [Mrs 'Barry Cornwall']. She shewed me one of her late husband's love-letters, date 1824. Also a photo of Henry James. She says he has made her an offer of marriage. Can it be so?

Thomas Hardy, 1880

An Engagement?

A life-long friend of Henry James and a witty woman from Boston, in speaking of him to me, said 'He has most noble qualities and is a sort of Massachusetts Sir Galahad.' I asked her why he had never married and she said he never wanted to, that he was once engaged to be married and when the lady broke it off he was so grateful to her that he became her devoted friend for life. 'He never,' she said, 'tempted Fate again. The next time the lady might not have been so kind.'

Mrs T. P. O'Connor

A Rumour

Mrs Edith Wharton told me that once at a dinner-party where Henry James was among the guests a message came from a newspaper asking her if she would verify a rumour. She read the message aloud to the assembled party — 'Are you and Henry James engaged to be married?' The silence was broken by Henry James, exclaiming 'And yet they say truth is stranger than fiction!'[1]

W. L. Phelps

Parisiennes

The austere and melancholy James . . . was ensconced in great splendour in the Rue de la Paix. James was positively decoyed once up into the Latin Quarter, and was to be seen by mortal eyes descending the Boulevard with a certain 'Reine de Golconde' on one arm and a certain 'Bobbinette' on the other.

Edmund Gosse, 1893

Much Beset

There was a general impression that Mr James was much beset by the attentions of ladies. One story dates from the days when

---

[1] A similarly false suspicion of James's romantic attachment for another American novelist, Elizabeth Jordan, is mentioned in the latter's *Three Rousing Cheers*. Mrs Belloc Lowndes has recorded the opinion that during his life in Europe James cared for only three women — Elizabeth Robins, Fanny Prothero and Rhoda Broughton.

domestic electric lighting was not yet fully under control. The first of the great London establishments to install the new luxury was, if I remember, Grosvenor House. At the subsequent evening party when the scene was at its most brilliant, suddenly the lights went out. As suddenly they came on, to discover — so the story went — thirteen ladies clinging to Mr James.

Elizabeth Robins

Sex Talk

In 1891 . . . [James] had a dachshund bitch with a beautiful countenance. He sat with the dachshund in his lap much of the time. We were speaking on the subject of sex in women and were comparing European women with American women in this regard. I had a notion that American women had less of this quality than European women, that in many American women it was negative, and in European women positive, and that many American girls looked like effeminate boys . . . James said, stroking the head of the dachshund: 'She's got sex, if you like, and she's quite intelligent enough to be shocked by this conversation.'

E. S. Nadal

Wantons

I have been staying at Rye with Henry James. He was telling me that some young actresses, staying at Winchelsea, had expressed a desire to see him and had come over to tea. I asked, 'Were they pretty?' He replied, 'Pretty! Good Heavens!!' and then, with the air of one who will be scrupulously just, he added: 'One of the poor wantons has a certain cadaverous grace.'

Edmund Gosse, 1899

Olga de Meyer

That enchanting Olga learnt more at Dieppe than my Maisie knew.

H. J., quoted by J.-E. Blanche

Goddess of Charity

In a corner formed by three folds of the Kien Lung screen, lighted by a Burmese chandelier of carved golden flowers and leaves that trailed downward over her head, I had placed a Chinese stone statue of the Goddess of Charity. Her right arm held in calm closeness to her side under gracious folds of modest raiment, her left hand outstretched to offer a basket filled with fruits of human kindness, eyes drooping to veil from sight the need of those who took, she stood for ever in impassioned serenity. It was to Henry James a source of unending wonder. Standing before it the first time he turned to me and chanted: 'Ah! my child, what a lesson to the artists of to-day on where to begin and to the women of to-day on where to leave off!'

Muriel Draper

A Compliment

I remember his coming in one day and meeting Mrs Frederick (afterwards Lady) Macmillan, to whom he paid a lengthy and involved compliment. When at last he paused for breath she replied, 'Dear Mr James, you always know exactly what to say to a woman.'

J. S. Bain

Eggs and Tangerines

Talking of someone we all knew, who was trailing round the provinces in company with a foreign actress and her apparently apathetic husband, James spoke of him as 'that foolish young man, with all his eggs, such as they are, in one poor basket.' On another occasion he mentioned a young couple 'who so intemperately squeezed out the juices of their inadequate tangerines.'

C. C. H. Millar

Recognition

I recall his story of how on his way down to the High Street he saw advancing towards him a woman whom he knew that he knew, but whom his racked memory failed to identify. As they drew fatally nearer each other she made a bee-line for him across the roadway and, still unidentified, opened conversation. 'I've had the rest of it,' she said, 'made into rissoles.' Recognition followed at once. 'And then in fact,' he said, 'the cudgelling of my brain ceased, for I recognized my own cook and knew that she was speaking of the leg of lamb I had eaten hot and roast on Monday and cold on Tuesday.'

E. F. Benson

CHILDREN

Trusted

Beloved Henry James! It seems to me that my original meeting with him was at the Andrew Langs in 1882. He was then forty-two[1] . . . Shortly after that Mr James came to see us in Russell Square, and a little incident happened which stamped itself for good on a still plastic memory. It was a very hot day; the western sun was beating on the drawing-room windows, though the room within was comparatively dark and cool. The children were languid with the heat and the youngest, Janet, then five, stole into the drawing-room and stood looking at Mr James. He put out a half-conscious hand to her; she came nearer, while we talked on. Presently she climbed on his knee. I suppose I made a maternal protest. He took no notice, and folded his arm round her. We talked on; and presently the abnormal stillness of Janet recalled her to me and made me look closely through the dark of the room. She was fast asleep, her pale little face on the young man's shoulder, her long hair streaming over his arm. Now Janet was a most independent and critical mortal, no indiscriminate 'climber up of knees'; far from it. Nor was Mr James an indiscriminate lover of children; he was not normally much at home

---

[1] James was under forty in 1882.

with them, though *always* good to them. But the childish instinct
had in fact divined the profound tenderness and chivalry which
were the very root of his nature; and he was touched and pleased,
as one is pleased when a robin perches on one's hand.

Mrs Humphry Ward

Our small boy . . . hated to be nursed by strangers. Mr Henry
James at once took him on his knee and forgot his existence, now
and then giving him an absent-minded squeeze while talking to
Conrad. We expected a petulant protest and a determined
wriggle to get away, but the child's tact, his instinctive sense of
Henry James's personality, surpassed our highest expectations.
He sat perfectly resigned and still for more than half an hour till
Mr James released him with a kiss.

Mrs Joseph Conrad

Understanding

He was . . . a very stately and courteous old gentleman; and, in
some social aspects especially, rather uniquely gracious. He
proved in one point that there was a truth in his cult of tact. He
was serious with children. I saw a little boy gravely present him
with a crushed and dirty dandelion. He bowed; but he did not
smile. That restraint was a better proof of the understanding of
children than the writing of *What Maisie Knew*.

G. K. Chesterton

Misunderstood

I remember once walking with him in the fields beyond Rye, and
two very small and grubby children opened the gate for us. He
smiled beneficently, felt in his deep pocket for coppers, found
some and then began an elaborate explanation of what the children were to buy. They were to go to a certain sweet shop because
there the sweets were better than at any other; they were to see

that they were not deceived and offered an inferior brand, for those particular sweets had a peculiar taste of nuts and honey with, he fancied, an especial flavour that was *almost* the molasses of his own country. If the children took care to visit the right shop and insisted that they should have only that particular sweet called, he fancied, 'Honey-nut' — or was it something with 'delight' in it? 'Rye's Delight' or 'Honey Delights' or — But at this moment the children, who had been listening open-mouthed, their eyes fixed on the pennies, of a sudden took fright and turned, running and roaring with terror across the fields.

He stood, bewildered, the pennies in his hand. What had he done? What had he said? He had meant nothing but kindness. Why had they run from him crying and screaming? He was greatly distressed, going over every possible corner of it in his mind. He alluded to it for days afterwards.

Hugh Walpole

Buttons

He asked to see my son, so that young person was sent for. The Irish [nurse] brought him. He was only a little over three years old and a few days before had been found asleep with a copy of Henry James's book *Letters* [sic] *of a Son and Brother* under his pillow, his hand slipped in at a page upon which a photograph of Henry and his brother William standing close to their father's knee was reproduced.[1] The tale of this incident had moved Henry James and when my son came into the room he fastened his accurately wise eye upon him. The Irish angel had brushed his hair until it shone and dressed him in his best afternoon raiment, which consisted of long linen trousers and suspenders cut out of one piece, fastened to a frilled white shirt at the shoulders by a huge pearl button. The devouring James focused his gaze on that

[1] There is no such photograph in *Notes of a Son and Brother*. The frontispiece in the earlier volume of reminiscence, *A Small Boy and Others*, shows Henry (but not William) standing with his hand on his father's shoulder.

button and held it there as the child crossed the vast room. Spontaneously glad to see this grown-up who in his youth had leaned so trustingly at his father's knee, my son had entered the room on the run, but faced with the arresting force of his gaze his footsteps faltered and his pace slackened, so that by the time he came to within three feet of Henry James he stopped short and remained motionless as that great man begin to address him:

'Ah! my boy. So here you come, faithfully — as it were, into view — with buttons, yes, *buttons* . . .' Here he paused while the yeast that would eventually give rise to the ultimate word began to ferment in the soles of his feet: as it reached his knees he repeated, 'Buttons, that are, er — that are — er — er . . .' By this time the poor child was intimidated by the intensity of tone and started to back away, but Henry James began a circular movement in air with the forefinger of his right hand and continued — 'buttons that have been — er' — and then in a shout of triumph — '*jettés-D*, as it were, yes, *jettés-d*' — his voice quieting down as the word emerged — '*jettés-d* so rightly, so needfully, just there, my child,' pointing in the direction of his small shoulder. But my child heard him not. At the first burst of '*jettés-D*' he had fled terrified from the room, the discovery of which brought forth from Henry James the mournful reflection, 'Would I had remained a photograph!'[1]

Muriel Draper

H. F. as Godfather

[James's letters to his god-daughter Dorothy Warren have been preserved but not published. One in 1897, in an envelope $2\frac{1}{2} \times 3\frac{3}{4}$ in.

[1] This anecdote recalls an incident in James's own childhood. He tells in *A Small Boy* how Thackeray, during his American lecture tour in 1852, visited the James household and distressed him by telling him that in England his extraordinary jacket would earn him the sobriquet 'Buttons'. The buttons, James once told Miss Jordan, 'covered me as stars cover the sky. I was dazzled by them. I expected Mr Thackeray to be dazzled too. But my buttons amused him and he laughed. It was a terrible experience for me. I have never forgotten it, for in that moment I experienced my first sense of disillusionment.' (Miss Jordan says that James at the time was six years of age, and that this was his sole meeting with Thackeray: he was in fact nine, and he also met Thackeray in Europe.)

enclosed with a doll, carried 'many, many, *ever* so many, loving little Xmas kisses' from 'Henrietta James'. Another — typewritten, long, complex yet designedly adapted to the mentality of a child — gave thanks for the 'very nice little *epistolary* mince-pie' which had made up to 'goddaddy' for his lack of proper Christmas fare in 1907.

Guy Millar in the following extracts was the grandson of George du Maurier and godson of Henry James. He had two brothers, Geoffrey and Gerald. 'George', in Mrs Comyns Carr's reminiscence, is perhaps a mistake for 'Guy'. The date of the first extract is about 1897.]

My dear Godson Guy, — I learned from your mother, by pressing her hard, some time ago that it would be a convenience to you and a great help in your career to possess an Association football — whereupon, in my desire that you should receive the precious object from no hand but mine I cast about me for the proper place to procure it. But I am living for the present in a tiny, simple-minded country town, where luxuries are few and football shops unheard of, so I was a long time getting a clue that would set me on the right road. Here at last, however, the result of my terribly belated endeavour. It goes to you by parcel post — not, naturally, in this letter. I am awfully afraid I haven't got one of the right size; if so, and you will let me know, you shall have a better one next time. I am afraid I don't *know* much about the sorts and sizes since they've all been invented since I was of football age. I'm an awful muff, too, at games — except at times I am not a bad cyclist, I think — and I fear I am only rather decent at playing at godfather. Some day you must come down and see me here and I'll do in every way the best I can for you. You shall have lots of breakfast and dinner and tea — not to speak of lunch and anything you like in between — and I won't ask you a single question about a single one of your studies, but if you think that is because I can't — because I don't know enough — I *might* get up subjects on purpose.

H. J. to Guy Millar

[The Millar boys] developed a sort of respect for Barrie because he was a cricketer. Not so with Henry James. 'George chose a cricket-ball for his birthday,' laughed the novelist to me, 'but he added,

"Take a man with you who knows what one's like." And he only accepted a theatre treat on condition the play should have some punch and not be one of your rotten high-brow affairs.'

Mrs J. Comyns Carr

Hearing that our eldest son Geoffrey had won a silver bowl, presented to the boy who had had most wins in the school sports, and that Guy had won a prize for throwing the cricket-ball, James wrote in letter to my wife from Rye as follows:

'I take in with great joy what you tell me of the school victories of the two boys, fabulous as it seems to me even to godfather a mighty thrower of balls. Please tell Guy that if I had known what further honours my connexion with him was going to bring me, I wouldn't have (as I did the other day) declined the honour of the vice-presidency of the Rye Cricket Club flatteringly pressed upon me. I am unworthy of such a descendant . . .'

No Christmas went by without Henry James sending some gift (generally books) to Geoffrey and Guy. Occasionally he wrote to Guy at school. One afternoon my wife found Guy 'and Jones minor' struggling in a corner of the cricket ground to decipher his latest.

C. C. H. Millar

ANIMALS

A Dog

He described a call he paid at dusk on some neighbours at Rye, how he rang the bell and nothing happened, how he rang again and again waited, how at the end there came steps in the passage and the door was slowly opened, and there appeared in advance on the threshold 'something black, something canine'.

E. F. Benson

A Cat

Settled in for the afternoon, surrounded by adoring ladies, the recluse of Rye sat complacent, holding my last new Persian kitten between his open palms, talking animatedly to the Beauty,[1] who could not talk but *looked*. He quite forgot the poor beast, which was too polite and too squeezed between the upper and the nether millstone of the great man's hands to remind him of its existence, and I dared not rescue it until the sentence on which Mr James was engaged was brought to a close — inside of half an hour.

Violet Hunt

A Canary

The conversation flagged; we were all a little shy. To ease the strain I praised his canary. Whereupon Henry James unclouded his dome brow and said, 'Yes, yes, the little creature sings his song of adoration each morning with — er — the slightest modicum of encouragement from me.'

C. Lewis Hind

[1 Violet Hunt's niece.]

OF PEOPLES

[The attitude of Henry James, a native American, to Europe, and of Henry James, a European by adoption, to America, is a subject co-extensive with his life. Its study is the study of his novels and short stories, his travel books, criticism and correspondence, and of a score or more of books and articles which others, particularly in America, have devoted to it. The few following extracts have been selected as character-istic from an embarrassment of available material.]

EUROPE

The English . . .

H. [said] one day that 'the English are the only people who can do great things without being clever'.

Alice James, 1891

. . . and the Germans

I wish you could have heard Henry James's lamentations over the British brain the other day in the Dresden Gallery. Of course only as regards things intellectual, otherwise it is a powerful instru-ment. So don't be offended. What made it so very comic is that he doesn't like the Germans — is affronted at their meals and the hours of their meals; their beds and their bedclothes; and their stoves and their sausages and their faces and their beer; so that their power of following ideas, which he was comparing with amazement to English incapacity, seemed to come in as an extra grievance against them — a way of adding insult to injury.

H. Brewster to E. Smyth, 1891

French and English

Harry . . . is just back from Paris, as amusing as ever about his experiences . . . English women, he says, look entirely different in Paris from what they do in London — not handsome, but big and clumsy . . .

I asked H. if the French *listen* as the English do: he said they all talk at once, like American women.

Alice James, 1889

The Daudets in London

[In May 1895 Alphonse Daudet and his wife and two sons visited London. Henry James constituted himself their cicerone. His letters record how he took them to see Windsor and to call on Meredith at Box Hill. Madame Daudet published a little book about the visit, *Notes sur Londres*, but apart from the dedication — *'A Henry James, Romancier: En souvenir du bon accueil'* — James is scarcely mentioned in it. Léon Daudet recorded his memories twenty years after the event.]

Nous étions logés dans Dover Street, en plein Piccadilly; mais chaque jour Henry James nous venait quérir pour une promenade, un thé, un déjeuner, un dîner, au club . . .

Alphonse Daudet l'aimait infiniment. Il lui disait un jour: 'Quel air de fierté ont les soldats anglais! Comme ils se cambrent pour marcher dans la rue, leur badine à la taille!' James répondit, la main en avant, avec ce débit scrupuleux et appuyé qui est le sien: 'Mon bon Daudet, il faut aussi, vous devez, il importe de tenir compte des servantes jeunes et jolies qui les observent derrière les carreaux.'

Je lui disais: 'Cher monsieur James, comment se fait-il que les Anglais fassent servir chez eux le vin, d'ailleurs excellent, dans des verres à liqueur et une seule fois à la fin du repas?' Il me répondit en riant: 'Cher monsieur Léon, cette antique coutume n'est heureusement pas universellement répandue. Vous êtes tombé jusqu'ici sur des hôtes de méthode œnophile archaïque, oui, terriblement archaïque.'

Nous nous amusions ainsi à relever les différences

fondamentales des tempéraments anglais et français, des habit-
udes de vie anglaises et françaises. Georges Hugo, qui est pas-
sionné pour l'Angleterre, soutenait toujours qu'ils avaient
raison, que c'était mieux ainsi, et James remettait gentiment les
choses au point: 'Cher monsieur Georges, tout n'est pas la perfection dans cette ancienne sympathique contradictoire civilisation.
Non, certes, tout n'y est pas parfait. Mais je suis heureux de vous
voir tenir pour agréable le petit repas du matin, avec ses délices
multiples et simples.' C'est-à-dire les poissons bien frais, le
jambon, les œufs, la confiture, tout le lest excellent de l'Anglais
qui part pour son travail.

Léon Daudet

Paris

I told him I was going on a first visit to Paris, and he warned me
against a possible disappointment. . . 'Do not,' he said, 'allow
yourself to be "put off" by the superficial and external aspect of
Paris; or rather (for the *true* superficial and external aspect of
Paris has a considerable fascination) by what I may call the superficial and external aspect *of* the superficial and external aspect of
Paris.' This was surely carrying lucidity to dazzling-point; I did
my best to profit by it, but I couldn't be sure that I was exercising
exactly the right discrimination, and in the end I surrendered to
the charm of Paris without too much circumspection.

Edward Marsh

France

The last time I saw him was, accidentally, in August of 1915 — on
the fourteenth of that month, in St James's Park. He said: 'Tu vas
te battre pour le sol sacré de Mme. de Staël!'

I suppose it was charactertistic that he should say 'de Mme. de
Staël' — and not of Stendhal, or even of George Sand! He
added — and how sincerely and with what passion — putting
one hand on his chest and just bowing, that he loved and had
loved France as he had never loved a woman.

F. M. Hueffer

. . . and Italy

'Why study France?' he demanded. 'France is only an imitation of Italy. Why waste time on the imitation when you can see the real thing?'

Hamlin Garland

Florence

Florence is the place in the world that I love the best, I think, and I should love it still better, I assure you, if it were to render you the solid service of putting you on your feet. I follow you, I accompany you, everywhere; but I just a little hope for you that the English colony won't tear you too much asunder. The English colony is the dark shade — in a general way — in the picture; and my fondness for the spot of earth is by no means because of them. However I permit you Lady Paget and her wondrous old Bellosguardo opera-box, as it strikes one, at the spectacle.

H. J. to E. Robins, 1901

Switzerland

'Always go to Switzerland alone,' said Henry James to me once. 'Company there is the least welcome distraction.'

H. M. Walbrook

The Belgians, 1915

He set down his tea-cup one afternoon in Logan [Pearsall Smith]'s drawing-room and declared in a voice that betrayed both the exasperation of the exhausted benefactor[1] and the relish of the phrase-maker: 'What is really tragic about them is that such an

[1] H. J. devoted much energy to the cause of the Belgian refugees in London in 1914–15 — so much indeed that ' "I think," said Mrs Cornish, "Henry James is a Belgian".'

uninteresting little nation should have found itself in such an interesting situation.'

James Whitall

AMERICA

[After he had settled in England in 1876 James paid only four visits, each of a few months, to America. The first two, in 1881–2 and 1882–3, were associated with the deaths of his mother and father; the last, in 1910–11, with that of his brother William. The third visit, 1904–5, was undertaken with the object of collecting material for his book *The American Scene*.]

Emigration

He had, in the 'sixties and early 'seventies, spent a long time [in America]. He told me that he had then given the country a 'good trial'.

E. S. Nadal

Homesick for England — First Visit . . .

We have had various people to tea and dinner every day. Thursday, Henry James put in an appearance; that young emigrant has much to learn here . . . He may in time get into the 'swim' here, but I doubt it. I think the real, live, vulgar, quick-paced world in America will fret him and that he prefers a quiet corner with a pen where he can create men and women who say neat things and have refined tastes and are not nasal or eccentric.

Mrs Henry Adams, 1882

Henry James has been in Washington for a month, very homesick for London.

Henry Adams, 1882

. . . Second Visit . . .

To-day Mr Henry James, writing from Boston, Massachusetts, under date of 27 January, speaks of his anticipated 'return to London from which, thank Heaven, my absence is only temporary'.

J. S. Bain, 1883

. . . Third Visit . . .

I am spending 5 days with Mrs Wharton, and this country (the motor helping) is of admirable beauty; but I am at the end of my long rope — the cord has snapped, and I long for (Sussex) repatriation.

H. J. to E. Robins, 1905

. . . Fourth Visit

Thanks to my still hanging rather on the fringe — the fringe *of* the fringe — of recovery (very difficult recovery) from a miserably long illness, I have just lately been rather unwell and unfit again . . . I think that what is the matter with me is mainly the desperate and temporarily frustrated desire to get back to dear old England again — so that I intensely *want* to believe that that is all that is needed for my steady re-establishment.

H. J. to Lady Macmillan, 1911

Damned Orchids

He found [his native country in 1904] greatly changed and was pained by many of the changes, which seemed to have borne out his worst forebodings. . . He disliked America's noise, the sloppy speech of its people, their bad manners and frequent rudeness . . . Most of all Mr James objected to what in an impassioned moment he called our 'damned orchids'. He seemed shocked by the oath even as it fell from his lips, but he made it clear that the 'damned orchids', which he seemed to be finding on every luncheon and dinner table where he sat as a guest, epitomized to him America's tendency toward vulgar ostentation.

In his turn he supplied Americans with a few disappointments. He remembered clearly and fondly the fine old literary guard of Boston and New York but he had no knowledge of or interest in the literary newcomers. While he was here I gave a reception for him, to which I invited his available old friends, as well as our best group of up-and-coming young writers. The names of the latter meant nothing to him, and his hearty handclasps did not comfort them for the revelation conveyed by his vague smile. Some of the writers, both old and young, resented this.

Elizabeth Jordan

Unmarketable Treasures

He hated [New York] as his letters abundantly testify; its aimless ugliness, its noisy irrelevance, wore on his nerves; but he was amused by the social scene, and eager to leave nothing of it unobserved. During his visits, therefore, we invited many people to the house, and he dined out frequently and went to the play — for he was still intensely interested in the theatre. But this mundane James, his attention scattered, his long and complex periods breaking against a dull wall of incomprehension, and dispersing themselves in nervous politenesses, was a totally different being from our leisurely companion at the Mount[1] . . . I remember depressing evenings when the hosts, contributing orchids and gold plate, remained totally unconscious of the royal gifts their guest had brought them in exchange.

James knew that his treasures were largely unmarketable in Fifth Avenue, but it perplexed and saddened him that they should, as a rule, be equally so in the world of letters, which he was naturally even more eager to explore. I remember one occasion when a dinner was especially arranged to make known to

---

[1] The Whartons' country house in Lenox, Massachusetts.

him a brilliant essayist whose books he greatly enjoyed. Unhappily the essayist's opaque countenance revealed nothing of the keenness within, and he on his part, though appreciative of James's genius, was obviously put off by his laborious hesitations. Their comments on the meeting were, on the essayist's side, a joke about James's stammer, and on James's the melancholy exclamation: 'What a mug!' . . .

At Cambridge, in the houses of his brother William James and of Charles Eliot Norton and their kindred circles, he had the best of Boston; and in Boston itself, where the sense of the past has always been so much stronger than in New York, he found all sorts of old affinities and relations and early Beacon Hill traditions to act as life-belts in the vast ocean of strangeness. He had always clung to his cousinage, and to anyone who represented old friendly associations, whether in Albany, New York or Boston, and I remember his once saying: 'You see, my dear, they're so much easier to talk to, because I can always ask them questions about uncles and aunts and other cousins.' He had brought this question-asking system to a high state of perfection, and practised it not only on relations and old friends, but on transatlantic pilgrims to Lamb House, whom he would literally silence by a friendly volley of interrogations as to what train they had taken to come down, and whether they had seen all the cathedral towns yet, and what plays they had done; so that they went away aglow with the great man's cordiality, 'and, you see, my dear, they hadn't time to talk to me about my books' — the calamity at all costs to be averted.

Edith Wharton

Recantation

'If I were to live my life over again,' he said in a low voice, and fixing upon me a sombre glance, 'I would be an American. I would steep myself in America, I would know no other land. I would study its beautiful side. The mixture of Europe and America which you see in me has proved disastrous. It has made of me a man who is neither American nor European. I have lost touch with my own people and I live here alone. My neighbours are friendly but they are not of my blood, except remotely. As a man grows old he feels these conditions more than when he is young. I shall never return to the United States,[1] but I wish I could.'

                                                              Hamlin Garland

Heat-Wave

[Refusing an invitation to Washington.]

I have a constitutional terror of hot weather — and the nature of the American summer had much to do with my flight from these shores long years ago. I shouldn't be a graceful guest or a crisp and finely starched ornament to your circle at all.

                                                    H. J. to Henry White, 1911

On one occasion his stay with us coincided with a protracted heat-wave; a wave of such unusual intensity that even the nights, usually cool and airy at the Mount, were as stifling as the days. My own dislike of heat filled me with sympathy for James, whose sufferings were acute and uncontrollable . . . During a heat-wave [his] curious inadaptability to conditions or situations became positively tragic. His bodily surface, already broad, seemed to expand to meet it, and his imagination to become a part of his body, so that the one dripped words of distress as the other did moisture. Always uneasy about his health, he became visibly anxious in hot weather, and this anxiety added so much to his sufferings that his state was pitiful. Electric fans, iced drinks and cold baths seemed to give no relief; and finally we discovered that the only panacea was incessant motoring. Luckily by that time

---

[1] He did. Mr Garland's visit to Rye was in 1906.

we had a car which would really go, and go we did, daily, incessantly, over miles and miles of lustrous landscape lying motionless under the still glaze of heat. While we were moving he was
refreshed and happy, his spirits rose, the twinkle returned to lips
and eyes; and we never halted except for tea on a high hillside or
for a 'cooling drink' at a village apothecary's — on one of which
occasions he instructed one of us to bring him 'something less
innocent than Apollinaris', and was enchanted when this was
interpreted as meaning an 'orange phosphate', a most sophisticated beverage for that day.

On another afternoon we had encamped for tea on a mossy
ledge in the shade of great trees, and as he seemed less uneasy
than usual somebody pulled out an anthology, and I asked one of
the party to read aloud Swinburne's 'Triumph of Time', which I
knew to be a favourite of James's; but after a stanza or two I saw
the twinkle of beatitude fade, and an agonized hand was lifted
up. 'Perhaps, in view of the abnormal state of the weather, our
young friend would have done better to choose a poem of less
inordinate length——' and immediately we were all bundled back
into the car and started off again on the incessant quest for air.

James was to leave for England in about a fortnight; but his
sufferings distressed me so much that, the day after this expedi-
tion, feeling sure that there was nothing to detain him in America
if he chose to go, I asked a friend who was staying in the house to
propose my telephoning for a passage on a Boston steamer which
was sailing within two days. My ambassador executed the commission and hurried back with the report that the mere hint of
such a plan had thrown James into a state of helpless per-
turbation. To change his sailing date at two days' notice — to get
from the Mount to Boston (four hours by train) in *two days* —
how could I lightly suggest anything so impracticable? And what
about his heavy luggage, which was at his brother William's in
New Hampshire? And his wash, which had been sent to the
laundry only the afternoon before? Between the electric fan
clutched in his hand and the pile of sucked oranges at his elbow he
cowered there, a mountain of misery, repeating in a sort of low
despairing chant: 'Good God, what a woman — what a woman!

Her imagination boggles at nothing! She does not even scruple to project me in a naked flight across the Atlantic . . .'

Edith Wharton

The Language

[John Sargent] told me, apropos of H. J.'s hatred of Americanisms, of a scene at which he had been present when a young American girl, being asked if she would have sugar with her tea, said: 'Oh, yes, please pass me the sugar basin and I will fix it.' On which H. J. with horror, 'My dear young lady, will you kindly tell me what you will fix it with, and what you will fix it to!'

John Bailey

Expatriates Meet

[Mr Whitall had been only a few months in England when he first met James, early in the 1914 war, in the house of Mrs P. L. Van Rensselaer.]

We were still standing, and when Mrs Van Rensselaer had begun to talk to my wife, thereby terminating the awkward silence that followed our four very British 'how d'you do's', I heard myself saying, 'I have shaken the dust of my country from my heels.'

The moment these words escaped me I knew that I had said enough to send him despairingly back to the chair from which he had so ponderously but so genially risen. He did not, however, do what this shockingly presumptuous introduction of a subject so closely woven into his personal and literary life gave him every excuse for doing. He came a step nearer and laid the burden of a heavy and meaningful hand upon my miserable shoulder . . .

'In speaking, my dear young man, as you have all frankly and all complacently spoken, you strike a note that, while I do full justice to the accomplished abandonment, sounds harshly to my ear; for though we may have done the beautifully right thing, though the wisdom of our choice be strikingly and unmistakably clear, we must never formulate anything, never allow our desire for approval to get, in our enjoyment of the achieved boon, the better of us.'

I remember having enough wind in my sails after this to tell Henry James that his friend Logan Pearsall Smith was my cousin and that reticence on the subject of quitting America was something I had seldom noticed in my talks with *him* . . .

'Ah, yes, poor dear good Logan!'

I tried to capture the significance of that little cluster of adjectives prefixed to Logan's name, but decided it had none beyond the intention to convey to me that Henry James had nothing further to say about expatriation . . .

When [James] arose once again from his comfortable chair there was a moment in which I feared a final crushing reference to my unfortunate assault upon his oversharpened sensibilities. But the import of the sentences whose laborious preparation had given me time for apprehension was as innocuous as their structure was complicated. He hoped — parenthetically, haltingly and with many restatements — that the dear lady would command the presence of us all in the near future, and 'he had been charmed'. As we made our way out into Church Street I could not help wondering whether there had not been after all a subtly veiled reprimand in his use of the flexible American formula when acknowledging our bleak British 'good-byes'.

James Whitall

CRITICISM AMONG FRIENDS

ADMINISTERED

In Henry James, revulsion from [bare] statements, when they might hurt, led him into periphrastic and metaphorical hesitations which by delaying a perhaps fatal verdict often made it in the end more crushing. Thus in conversation when he had done speaking one was sometimes reminded of that comment upon Renan: *'le plus doux des hommes cruels.'* And yet Henry James was not cruel. He had a merciless eye and a tender heart, and in a style of delicate and prolonged ingenuity he strove to combine the reports of the one with the promptings of the other.

Desmond MacCarthy

I remember a painful moment during one of his visits when my husband imprudently blurted out an allusion to 'Edith's new story — you've seen it in the last *Scribner*?' . . . He instantly replied: 'Oh, yes, my dear Edward, I've read the little work — of course I've read it.' A gentle pause, which I knew boded no good; then he softly continued: 'Admirable, admirable; a masterly little achievement.' He turned to me, full of a terrifying benevolence. 'Of course so accomplished a mistress of the art would not, without deliberate intention, have given the tale so curiously conventional a treatment. Though indeed, in the given case, no treatment *but* the conventional was possible; which might conceivably, my dear lady, on further consideration, have led you to reject your subject as — er — in itself a totally unsuitable one.'

I will not deny that he may have added a silent twinkle to the shout of laughter with which . . . his fellow guests greeted my 'dressing-down'. Yet it would be a mistake to imagine that he had deliberately started out to destroy my wretched tale. He had begun, I am sure, with the sincere intention of praising it; but no sooner had he opened his lips than he was overmastered by the need to speak the truth, and the whole truth, about anything connected with the art which was sacred to him . . . His tender regard for his friends' feelings was equalled only by the faithfulness with which, on literary questions, he gave them his view of their case when they asked for it — and sometimes when they did not. On all subjects but that of letters his sincerity was tempered by an almost exaggerated tenderness; but when *le métier* was in question no gentler emotion prevailed.

Another day — somewhat later in our friendship, since this time the work under his scalpel was *The Custom of the Country* — after prolonged and really generous praise of my book he suddenly and irrepressibly burst forth: 'But of course you know — as how should you, with your infernal keenness of perception, *not* know? — that in doing your tale you had under your hand a magnificent subject, which ought to have been your main theme, and that you used it as a mere incident and then passed it by?' . . .

Once when he was staying with us in Paris I had a still more amusing experience of this irresistible tendency to speak the truth. He had chanced to nose out the fact that responding to an S.O.S. from the *Revue des Deux Mondes*, for a given number of which a promised translation of one of my tales had not been ready, I had offered to replace it by writing a story[1] myself — in French! I knew what James would feel about such an experiment, and there was nothing I did not do to conceal the horrid secret from him; but he had found it out before arriving, and when in my presence some idiot challenged him with: 'Well, Mr James, don't you think it's remarkable that Mrs Wharton should have written a story in French for the *Revue*?' the twinkle which began in the corner of his eyes and trickled slowly down to his twitching lips shewed that his answer was ready. 'Remarkable — most remarkable! An altogether astonishing feat.' He swung around on me slowly. 'I do congratulate you, my dear, on the way in

[1 'Les Metteurs-en-scène,' *Revue des Deux Mondes*, 1 August 1908.]

which you've picked up every old worn-out literary phrase that's been lying about the streets of Paris for the last twenty years, and managed to pack them all into those few pages.' To this withering comment, in talking over the story afterward with one of my friends, he added more seriously, and with singular good sense: 'A very creditable episode in her career. *But she must never do it again.*'

Edith Wharton

WITHHELD

The tale — perhaps the most beautiful of his later short stories — called 'The Velvet Glove' . . . was suggested by the fact that a very beautiful young Englishwoman of great position, and unappeased literary ambitions, had once tried to beguile him into contributing an introduction to a novel she was writing — or else into reviewing the book; I forget which. She had sought from him, at any rate, a literary 'boost' which all his admiration and liking for her could not, he thought, justify his giving; and they parted, though still friends, with evidences on her part of visible disappointment — and surprise.

Edith Wharton

J'essaierai de rendre, moins les *euh . . . euh . . .* , [une phrase] d'Henry James à mademoiselle X, qui s'était enhardie à lui montrer un manuscrit:

'Chère enfant — si je puis ainsi vous appeler, maintenant encore . . . quoique, en vérité, pour moi tout le monde soit un enfant . . . et puisque vous avez atteint déjà à une célébrité que Edith Wharton — oh! notre admirable, stupéfiante Edith![1] — mais avez-vous publié? Oui, sans

---

[1] 'I have never met Mrs Wharton and I know that she is a delightful lady, but oh! how in those young days I learnt to loathe her very name! . . . My *naïvetés* were exposed naked to her sophisticated wisdom — all this in the kindliest fashion. But the kindliness only made me hate her image the more. Had it been a century or two earlier I would have made a doll of wax, named it Wharton, stuck pins into it and roasted it over a slow fire.' — *Hugh Walpole.*

doute quelque fleur rare de votre ravissant (*comely*) jardin de lettres, dans un de ces détestables périodiques de notre chère mère-patrie, lesquels je ne lis jamais, oh! non pas que ces pléthoriques emporiums de l'universelle information ne renferment des perles parmis le fumier (*rubbish*) — mais à vrai dire le temps me manque, à moi qui suis sur le sombre versant, même pour accueillir un manuscrit . . . — et puisque, donc, la rumeur de votre jeune génie se propage jusqu'au seuil de ma retraite (nécessaire mais subie — oh! bien douce quand elle ne me gruge pas d'occasions incomparables telles que celle-ci, de votre rencontre, chère enfant!) Eh bien! eh bien! (*Well, well!*) l'envie, la curiosité passionnée que j'éprouve de m'introduire dans le tabernacle de votre auguste sanctuaire (un nouveau culte impliquant toujours un nouveau héros), j'accepte de recevoir de vos mains, mon enfant, cet inestimable cahier — sans toutefois être sûr de ne devoir vous le rendre avant de l'avoir savouré plus que tant d'autres à moi confiés par d'autres écrivains, oh! bien malgré moi . . . bien malgré moi.'

Le manuscrit ne fut pas confié au maître. Celui-ci m'assura qu'il avait regretté de ne s'être point mieux fait comprendre de la demoiselle; il en fut peiné et profondément blessé.

J.-E. Blanche

RECEIVED

Modestly

[Of his review of Stevenson's Letters in the *North American Review*.]

You are quite right — wholly — about my being in places too entortillé. I am *always* in places too entortillé — and the effort of my scant remaining years is to make the places fewer.

H. J. to S. Colvin, 1900

Tartly

. . . the deserved rebuke I overheard Mr James give a woman who was foolish enough to ask the Master the meaning of a certain passage in *The Wings of the Dove*.

'My dear lady,' Mr James said coldly, 'if after the infinite labour I give to my literature I am unable to convey to you my meaning, how can you expect me to do so by mere word of mouth?'

Elizabeth Jordan

With Pained Surprise

I brought him in all innocence a passage from one of his books which, after repeated readings, I still found unintelligible. He took the book from me, read over the passage to himself, and handed it back with a lame attempt at a joke; but I saw — we all saw — that even this slight and quite involuntary criticism had wounded his morbidly delicate sensibility.

Once again — and again unintentionally — I was guilty of a similar blunder. I was naturally much interested in James's technical theories and experiments, though I thought, and still think, that he tended to sacrifice to them that spontaneity which is the life of fiction . . . His latest novels, for all their profound moral beauty, seemed to me more and more lacking in atmosphere, more and more severed from that thick nourishing human air in which we all live and move. The characters in *The Wings of the Dove* and *The Golden Bowl* seem isolated in a Crookes tube for our inspection: his stage was cleared like that of the Théâtre Français in the good old days when no chair or table was introduced that was not *relevant to the action* (a good rule for the stage, but an unnecessary embarrassment to fiction). Preoccupied by this, I one day said to him: 'What was your idea in suspending the four principal characters in *The Golden Bowl* in the void? What sort of life did they lead when they were not watching each other, and fencing with each other? Why have you stripped them of all the *human fringes* we necessarily trail after us through life?'

He looked at me in surprise, and I saw at once that the surprise was painful and wished I had not spoken. I had assumed that his system was a deliberate one, carefully thought out, and had been genuinely anxious to hear his reasons. But after a pause of reflection he answered in a disturbed voice: 'My dear — I didn't know I had!' and I saw that my question, instead of starting one of our absorbing literary discussions, had only turned his startled attention on a peculiarity of which he had been completely unconscious.

Edith Wharton

The Great Revision

All through the quiet autumn and winter of 1906 he was busy preparing the collective and definite, but far from complete, edition of his novels and tales which began to appear some twelve months later. This involved a labour which some of his friends ventured to disapprove of, since it included a re-writing into his latest style of the early stories which possessed a charm in their unaffected immaturity. Henry James was conscious, I think, of the arguments which might be brought against this reckless revision, but he rejected them with violence. I was spending a day or two with him at Lamb House when *Roderick Hudson* was undergoing, or rather had just undergone, the terrible trial; so the revised copy, darkened and swelled with MS alterations, was put into my hands. I thought — I dare say I was quite mistaken — that the whole perspective of Henry James's work, the evidence of his development and evolution, his historical growth, were confused and belied by this wholesale tampering with the original text. Accordingly I exclaimed against such dribbling of new wine into the old bottles. This was after dinner, as we sat alone in the garden-room. All that Henry James — though, I confess, with a darkened countenance — said at the time was, 'The only alternative would have been to put the vile thing' — that is to say the graceful tale of *Roderick Hudson* — 'behind the fire and have done with it!' Then we passed to other subjects, and at length we parted for the night in unruffled cheerfulness. But what was my dismay, on reaching the breakfast-table next morning, to see my host sombre and taciturn, with gloom thrown across his frowning features like a veil. I inquired rather anxiously whether he had slept well. 'Slept!' he answered with dreary emphasis. 'Was I likely to sleep when my brain was tortured with all the cruel and — to put it plainly to you — monstrous insinuations which you had brought forward against my proper, my necessary, my absolutely inevitable corrections of the disgraceful and disreputable style of *Roderick Hudson*?'

                                                        Edmund Gosse

[A more temperate reply to a young American who had ventured a criticism similar to Gosse's will be found in Robert Herrick's 'A Visit to Henry James', and a penetrating first-hand account of the work of revising the novels is given in *Henry James at Work* by his secretary, Miss Bosanquet, from which there is space only to quote:]

On a morning when he was obliged to give time to the selection of a set of tales for a forthcoming volume he confessed that the difficulty of selection was mainly the difficulty of reading them at all. 'They seem,' he said, 'so bad until I *have* read them that I can't force myself to go through them except with a pen in my hand, altering as I go the crudities and ineptitudes that to my sense deform each page.' . .

He knew he could write better. His readers have not always agreed with his own view. They have denounced the multiplication of qualifying clauses, the imposition of a system of punctuation which, although rigid and orderly, occasionally fails to act as a guide to immediate comprehension of the writer's intention, and the increasing passion for adverbial interpositions. 'Adjectives are the sugar of literature and adverbs the salt,' was Henry James's reply to a criticism which once came to his ears.

                                                        Theodora Bosanquet

[James's final word on the great revision was spoken in 1914.]

I was telling him that it was my intention to rewrite *Carnival* and get rid of what I now thought were mistakes of treatment. The massive face of Henry James looked what must be called horror-stricken . . .

'I wasted months of labour upon the thankless, the sterile, the preposterous, the monstrous task of revision. There is not an hour of such labour that I have not regretted since. You have been granted the most precious gift that can be granted to a young writer — the ability to toss up a ball against the wall of life and catch it securely at the first rebound. You have that ability to an altogether unusual extent. None of your contemporaries, so far as I have knowledge of their work, enjoys such an immediate and direct impact, and of those in the generation before you only H. G. Wells. It is a wonderful gift but it is a dangerous gift, and I entreat you, my dear boy, to beware of that immediate and direct return of the ball into your hands, while at the same time you rejoice in it.

'I, on the contrary, am compelled to toss the ball so that it travels from wall to wall . . .' here with a gesture he seemed to indicate that he was standing in a titanic fives-court, following with anxious eyes the ball he had just tossed against the wall of life . . . 'from wall to wall until at last, losing momentum with every new angle from which it rebounds, the ball returns to earth and dribbles slowly to my feet, when I arduously bend over, all my bones creaking, and with infinite difficulty manage to reach it and pick it up.'

Compton Mackenzie

Parodied

Still more disastrous was the effect of letting him know that any of his writings had been parodied. I had always regarded the fact of being parodied as one of the surest evidences of fame, and once, when he was staying with us in New York, I brought him with glee a deliciously droll article on his novels by poor Frank Colby, the author of *Imaginary Obligations* [1904]. The effect was disastrous. I shall never forget the misery, the mortification even, which tried to conceal itself behind an air of offended dignity. His ever-bubbling sense of fun failed him completely on such occasions.

Edith Wharton

My Dear Max, — Henry James has been eating his Christmas dinner here with us, and I am anxious to let you know that he started the subject of your *Christmas Garland*, and discussed it with the most extraordinary vivacity and appreciation. He was full of admiration. I told him that you had a certain nervousness about his acceptance of your parody of him, and he desired me to let you know at once that no one can have read it with more wonder and delight than he.[1]

Edmund Gosse, 1913

[1] Max Beerbohm's *Christmas Garland* contains parodies of a number of leading writers of the day: that of James is called 'The Mote in the Middle Distance'. Two months later Gosse told Siegfried Sassoon that James had roamed round the room discussing, 'with extraordinary vivacity and appreciation, not only the superlative intelligence of the book as a whole but 'The Mote in the Middle Distance' itself, which he had read in a self-scrutinizing bewilderment of wonder and admiration'.

PUBLIC AND PRIVATE

THE PROFESSIONS

Politics

He talked of politics, the immense waste of talk and energy and solemnity that Parliament is. He often wondered how so complex and cumbrous as machine as the British Empire managed to go on at all; there must be some mysterious tough element in it; perhaps it was easier for it to go on than to stop. The older he grew the more acutely and passionately did he feel the huge absurdity and grotesqueness of things, the monstrous perversity of evil. His taste became more and more delicate and sensitive. On my wondering why anyone should attach importance to *taste*, 'Attach importance!' he burst out, 'that isn't what one ever does or did to it. Why, it attaches importance to one!'[1] He felt tempted to call himself a rabid Socialist, so often does a great wind carry him off his feet and set him down somewhere far beyond and ahead of the present world.

S. P. Waterlow, 1907

The Church

James shook his enormous head gravely and sadly as he replied: 'Intolerance is of the devil, and yet, contradictorily enough, it often appears to me to be the outstanding characteristic of the Church and the priestly mind.' [He read aloud a passage from the *Lectures on Anglican Difficulties*.] 'I did not think it could have been possible,' he continued, 'to produce such an incredible

[1 '. . . to one', emended from '. . . to me'.]

instance of exaggeration as is contained in this almost insane sentence by John Henry Newman' . . . 'I would like,' continued Mr James, 'to make a really scientific study of the whole history of religious intolerance, which is, I really believe, the history of humanity.'

Raymond Blathwayt

. . . and the Stage

[Gerald du Maurier's parents were not in favour of his adopting the stage as a career.]

One afternoon they were discussing the position with Henry James, who said that if Gerald really wanted to go on the stage he didn't see how they could prevent it. 'That's all very well, James; but what would you say if you had a son who wanted to go into the Church?' Lifting both hands in horror Henry James replied, 'My dear du Maurier, a father's curse!'

C. C. H. Millar

The Press

[In January 1886 Edward Cook, assistant editor of the *Pall Mall Magazine*, invited a number of distinguished persons to submit lists of 'the hundred best books'.]

Mr Henry James's letter . . . ran thus:

'I must beg you to excuse me from sending you, as you do me the honour to propose, a list of the hundred best books. I have but few convictions on this subject, and they may indeed be resolved into a single one, which, however, may not decently be reproduced in the columns of a newspaper, [and] which for reasons apart from its intrinsic value (be that great or small) I do not desire to see made public. It is simply that the reading of the newspapers is *the* pernicious habit and the father of all idleness and levity . . .'

Mr James, to his 'great alarm and surprise', received a proof of this letter the following day, and had to appeal to the editor's 'fine sense of honour' not to let it appear.

J. Saxon Mills

Pure English

[As a pendant to James's refusal of Cook's request may be added his qualified refusal to join the Society for Pure English.]

I am . . . moved to plead with you, by a single word, to the effect of your not too earnestly *counting* on me to join by public appearance in your lingual manifesto — for I have never joined in any sort of manifesto or signed public pronouncement that I can recollect, in the whole course of my life, and greatly hang back from any new departure in that connexion at this late day — oh so very late as I feel it to be. 'It isn't my way' — and what *is* my way (as a poor, lonely, and independent old artist-man) is so very different. If one has the good fortune to be a p.1. and i.o a.-m. *that* and that only is one's form, and a form beyond any falling into line with the Raleighs, Mackails, and *tutti quanti*. Which doesn't mean, however, my dear Logan and my dear Bridges, that I don't find your reaching-forth very interesting and discussable, even though I think you rush into a sandy Sahara of an extent you can have no conception of, if you haven't (and I think you haven't!) lately been to America. It will be none the less — all the more — jolly to talk!

H. J. to R. Bridges and L. P. Smith, 1913

THE PRIVATE LIFE

The Lamp at the Window

[The experience confided to Gosse was confided also to Hugh Walpole, who says that it occurred in James's youth in a foreign town. Walpole tells the story as an illustration of the view that James had suffered some sexual frustration.]

So discreet was he, and so like a fountain sealed, that many of those who were well acquainted with him have supposed that he was mainly a creature of observation and fancy, and that life stirred his intellect while leaving his senses untouched. But every now and then he disclosed to a friend, or rather admitted such a friend to a flash or glimpse of, deeper things. The glimpse was never prolonged or illuminated, it was like peering down for a moment through some chasm in the rocks dimmed by the vapour of a clash of waves. One such flash will always leave my memory dazzled. I was staying alone with Henry James at Rye one summer and as twilight deepened we walked together in the garden. I forget by what meanders we approached the subject, but I suddenly found that in profuse and enigmatic language he was recounting to me an experience, something that had happened, not something repeated or imagined. He spoke of standing on the pavement of a city, in the dusk, and of gazing upwards across the misty street, watching, watching for the lighting of a lamp in a window on the third storey. And the lamp blazed out, and through bursting tears he strained to see what was behind it, the unapproachable face. And for hours he stood there, wet with the rain, brushed by the phantom hurrying figures of the scene, and never from behind the lamp was for one moment visible the face. The mysterious and poignant revelation closed, and one could make no comment, ask no question, being throttled oneself by an overpowering emotion. And for a long time Henry James shuffled beside me in the darkness, shaking the dew off the laurels, and still there was no sound at all in the garden but what our heels made crunching the gravel, nor was the silence broken when suddenly we entered the house and he disappeared for an hour.

Edmund Gosse

H. J. as Brother

[Alice James was a chronic but indomitable invalid, Henry a devotedly attentive brother. At the time of the first of the following extracts she was bed-ridden in 'rooms' in Leamington and William James had lately arrived in England.]

I must try and pull myself together and record the somewhat devastating episode of 18 July when Harry, after a much longer absence than usual, presented himself, doubled by William! We had just finished luncheon and were talking of something or other when H. suddenly said, with a queer look upon his face, 'I must tell you something.' 'You're not going to be married!' shrieked I. 'No, but William is here; he has been lunching upon Warwick Castle, and is waiting now in the Holly Walk for the news to be broken to you; and if you survive I'm to tie my handkerchief to the balcony.' Enter W., not à la Romeo, by the balcony; the prose of our century, to say nothing of our consanguinity, making it supererogatory. The beforehand having been so cleverly suppressed by the devoted H., 'it came out so much easier than could have been expected,' as they say to infants in the dental chair . . . Poor H., over whom the moment had impended for two months, looked as white as a ghost before they went; and well he may, in his anxiety as to which 'going off' in my large repertory would 'come on'; but, with the assistance of two hundred grains of bromide, I think I behaved with extreme propriety . . .

Henry came on [10 March] to spend the day; Henry the Patient I should call him. Five years ago, in November, I crossed the water and suspended myself like an old woman of the sea round his neck, where to all appearances I shall remain for all time. I have given him endless care and anxiety, but notwithstanding this and the fantastic nature of my troubles I have never seen an impatient look upon his face or heard an unsympathetic or misunderstanding sound cross his lips. He comes at my slightest sign and 'hangs on' to whatever organ may be in eruption, and gives me calm and solace by assuring me that my nerves are his nerves, and my stomch his stomach — this last a pitch of brotherly devotion never before approached by the race. He has never remotely hinted that he expected me to be well at any given moment — that burden which fond friend and relative so inevitably impose upon the cherished invalid. But he has always been the same since I can remember, and has almost as strongly as Father that personal susceptibility, what can one call it — it seems as if it were a matter of the scarfskin, as if they perceived through that your mood, and were saved thereby from rubbing you raw with their theory of it or blindness to it . . .

H. was also here 15 April. It is so reposeful to see him. He is so unsuggestive as to the conduct of life, the angle of one's cushions, or the number of one's shawls.

Alice James, 1889–90

His love for his own relations, his brother William, his nephew, had a real pathos, for although they beautifully returned it they could never be so deeply absorbed in him as he was in them. I went once to Brown's Hotel to say good-bye to him before his departure for America with William James who was very ill. While I was with him a message came and he hurried away. I waited and waited but no one came, so at last I started downstairs. I passed an open bedroom door and saw William lying on the floor and Henry standing over him. As I hurried down I caught an expression of misery and despair on Henry's face that I shall never forget.

Hugh Walpole

Disconcerting Incidents

[Many writers have alluded to James's avoidance of 'disconcerting incidents', whether these occurred in works of art or the private affairs of his friends. This characteristic is not easy to illustrate by anecdotes. There is an illuminating passage in Mr Forrest Reid's *Private Road* describing James's 'chilly' reception of *The Garden God*, but it does not lend itself to extraction. One way in which James signified his displeasure with Mr Reid as with Violet Hunt (page 151 below), was by exchanging an affectionate for a more formal address at the beginning of a letter: 'It was plain that I was no longer anybody's "dear young man".' Mr Reid quotes:]

[James] once called on the Beardsleys and Aubrey's sister (a beautiful and charming girl) pointed out to him on the stairs a Japanese print which shocked him. He called it a 'disconcerting incident' and always afterwards fought shy of her, though the print on the stairs was nothing startling. I remember once teasing him with a friend to know what the Olympian young man in 'In the Cage' had done wrong. He swore he did not know, he would rather not know.

André Raffalovich

I remember once saying to Henry James, in reference to a novel of the type that used euphemistically to be called 'unpleasant': 'You know, I was rather disappointed; that book wasn't nearly as bad as I expected;' to which he replied with his incomparable twinkle: 'Ah, my dear, the abysses are all so shallow.'

Edith Wharton

Lost Weekend[1]

Henry James was ill. I wrote to him, and received in return a letter combining the suavity of the host with the touchiness of the invalid:

October 31st, 1909.

My dear Violet, — Yes, indeed, I am at Rye — where else should I be? For I am here pretty well always and ever, and less and less anywhere else. There are advantages preponderant in that; but there are also drawbacks; one of which is that I am liable to go so long without seeing you. But to this, on the other hand, there are possible remedies — as, for instance, that of your conceivably (I hope) coming down here for a couple of nights before very long . . . The *week-end* would suit me (though I am not restricted to that) of almost any of the next weeks . . .

I accepted with the usual heartily expressed elation — that was merely respect — but I think I really rather loved Henry James; I had known him so long, and as a plastic schoolgirl. But it was not

---

[1] Violet Hunt's account of this incident occupies seven pages of *The Flurried Years*. For convenience in reading many of the excisions are not here indicated in the narrative paragraphs; they are however indicated in James's letters.

to be. My pitch was queered damnably. There had been signs, rumblings.[1] And a week after I had accepted I received letters from Henry James which decidedly knocked the first nail into my coffin. For observe the change of title — a change subtle and cruel!

Dear Violet Hunt, — I should be writing to you to-night to say that it would give me great pleasure to see you on Saturday next had I not received by the same post which brought me your letter one from——, which your mention of the fact that you have known the writing of it enables me thus to allude to as depriving, by its contents, our projected occasion of indispensable elements of frankness and pleasantness. I deeply lament and deplore the lamentable position in which I gather you have put yourself . . . It affects me as painfully unedifying, and that compels me to regard all agreeable or unembarrassed communications between us as impossible. I can neither suffer you to come down to hear me utter those homely truths, nor pretend at such a time to free or natural discourse of other things on a basis of avoidance of what must now be most to the front in your own consciousness, or what in a very unwelcome fashion disconcerts mine. Otherwise, *'es wäre so schön gewesen!'* But I think you will understand, on a moment's further reflection, that I can't write to you otherwise than I do, or that I am very sorry indeed to have to do it.

　　Believe me, then, in very imperfect sympathy,
　　　　Yours,
　　　　　HENRY JAMES.

I wrote, and he replied:

. . . I am obliged to you for your letter of Wednesday last, but, with all due consideration for it, I do not see, I am bound to tell you, that it at all invalidates my previous basis of expression to you. It appeared from that . . . that the person best qualified to measure the danger feared for your reputation, and I really don't see how an old friend of yours *could* feel or pronounce your being in a position to permit of this anything but lamentable, lamentable, oh, lamentable! . . . I, however, deprecate the discussion of private affairs of which I wish to hear nothing whatever. And, neither knowing or willing to know anything of the matter, it was

---

[1] The 'rumblings' concerned Violet Hunt's association with F. M. Hueffer and impending proceedings against him by his wife.

exactly because I didn't wish to that I found conversing with you at all to be in prospect impossible. That was the light in which I didn't — your term is harsh! — *forbid* you my house; but deprecated the idea of what would otherwise have been so interesting and welcome a *tête-à-tête* with you. I am very sorry to have had to lose it, and I am yours in regret,

HENRY JAMES.

November 5th, 1909.

Then I wrote to my dear Henry James passionately, speaking for myself, declaring that, for my part, I wasn't in a 'lamentable position' at all. I assured him in plain language, using the stock, stereotyped expression consecrated by long use, that I was 'innocent', and could not be dragged into anything. One knew that the one thing Henry really dreaded was being mixed up with life in any way, or entangled in anything that went on outside the drawing-room door. Later, ashamed of what I will call his *inburst*, he confessed to Mrs P. that he 'had simply kept out of it because I am too old to be mixed up in messes.' . . .

He had been ill again, and I had written to inquire. He replied [on 14 February 1910]. I was 'Dear Violet' again!

Violet Hunt

THE NOVELIST

THE SOLITUDE OF GENIUS

It was just about this period that my fellow expatriate Henry James was writing his best short stories; and in the year my little book [*The Youth of Parnassus*, 1895] was published appeared the volume called *Terminations*, in which are contained three at least of his masterpieces . . . I sent this master, with whom I was slightly acquainted, my little book; he mislaid it in the Underground, and after some weeks he wrote a letter full of apologies in which he told me that he had procured another copy, and asked me to come and see him and talk the book over. Of course I went. Henry James was to me then but a revered master, not the friend he became afterwards, and I listened with reverent ears to what he said about my stories. His praise was kindly but tepid; I think he saw the gift for story writing was not my gift; and, as he said in another connexion, although one may lie about anything else, about matters of art one doesn't lie.

About the profession of letters in general, the desire to do the best one could with one's pen — and this I confessed was my ambition — he made one remark which I have never forgotten. 'My young friend,' he said, 'and I call you young — you are disgustingly and, if I may be allowed to say so, nauseatingly young — there is one thing that, if you really intend to follow the course you indicate, I cannot too emphatically insist on. There is one word — let me impress upon you — which you must inscribe upon your banner, and that,' he added after an impressive pause, 'that word is *Loneliness*.'

Logan Pearsall Smith

After a luncheon party of which he had been, as they say, 'the life', we happened to be drinking our coffee together while the rest of the party had moved on to the verandah. 'What a charming picture they make,' he said, with his great head aslant, 'the women there with their embroidery, the . . .' There was nothing in his words, anybody might have spoken them; but in his attitude, in his voice, in his whole being at that moment, I divined such complete detachment that I was startled into speaking out of myself. 'I can't bear to look at life like that,' I blurted out, 'I want to be in everything. Perhaps that is why I cannot *write*, it makes me feel absolutely alone . . .' The effect of this confession upon him was instantaneous and surprising. He leant forward and grasped my arm excitedly: 'Yes, it is solitude. If it runs after you and catches you, well and good. But for heaven's sake don't run after *it*. It is absolute solitude.' And he got up hurriedly and joined the others.

On the walk home it occurred to me that I had for a moment caught a glimpse of his intensively private life, and rightly or wrongly I thought that this glimpse explained much: his apprehensively tender clutch upon others, his immense preoccupation with the surface of things and his exclusive devotion to his art. His confidence in himself in relation to that art I thought I discerned one brilliant summer night as we were sauntering along a dusty road which crosses the Romney marshes. He had been describing to me the spiral of depression which a recent nervous illness had compelled him step after step, night after night, day after day, to descend. He would, he thought, never have found his way up again had it not been for a life-line thrown to him by his brother William; perhaps the only man in whom he admired equally both heart and intellect. What stages of arid rejection of life and meaningless yet frantic agitation he had been compelled to traverse! 'But,' and he suddenly stood still, 'but it has been good' — and here he took off his hat, baring his great head in the moonlight — 'for my genius.' Then, putting on his hat again, he added 'Never cease to watch whatever happens to you.'

Desmond MacCarthy

He counselled me, 'It's a great honour to be allowed to dream even that we may find a chance to produce a little life that is exempt from the law of extinction — not at the mercy of accident. Live your life and stick to your table. Be a patient woman and a ferocious artist, and try to combine that mildness and that firmness. Nothing has helped me really but *Time* . . . and friendly response.'

Olivia Garnett

FINDING COPY

Family Plagiarism

H., by the way, has embodied in his pages many jewels fallen from my lips, which he steals in the most unblushing way, saying simply that he knew they had been said by the family, so it did not matter.

Alice James, 1891

'Germs'

The doyen of the [*English*] *Review*, Henry James, lived mostly in London now, 'chaperoning himself'. *Modeste Mignon*, I called him, after Balzac. He never, so far as I know, honoured the office — which was also a drawing-room — with his presence . . . But he used to come to see me in my house, nicely *montée* for entertaining, and to any one of my three clubs. He delighted in my Saturdays at the Socialist New Reform Club, where the members consumed eggs beaten up in glasses . . .

It was quite unnecessary to be careful to whom you introduced H. J. . . . Nobody bored him; he took care of that . . . I used to suffer, as other people did who told him anything that might amuse him, from the summarily truncated anecdote. He would hold up a story as soon as he had got all he needed out of it; extend a finger — 'Thank you, I've got as much — all I want' — and leave you with the point of your anecdote on your hands.[1]

Violet Hunt

The Sense of the Past

In the early months of the War I was invited suddenly, and a little peremptorily, by Edmund Gosse to dine with him at the National Club (in Whitehall Gardens) — to meet the Prime Minister and Henry James . . . The party numbered eight in all, but when I had greeted my host in front of the fire I was at once button-holed — or more literally 'lapel-held' — by Henry James, who spun for me so rapid and flattering and bewildering a thread that I lost consciousness of everything else that was going on, and we at last awoke to the fact that the rest of the company had gone in to dinner without us . . .

[After dinner James] to my surprise turned to me with a renewal of his complimentary remarks on my prose work, which showed me that he had *The Old Country* still freshly in mind though it was by this time eight years old. The meaning of this remained obscure to me until 1917, when I read after Henry James's death his unfinished volume called *The Sense of the Past*. In that I found the evidences of an analysis, to me at any rate most interesting, of the motifs and situations devised by me for my story and afterwards used or adapted by him for his own book.[2]

Henry Newbolt

---

[1] Cf. Introduction to *The Spoils of Poynton* (1908). 'It was years ago, I remember, one Christmas Eve when I was dining with friends: a lady beside me made in the course of talk one of those allusions that I have always found myself recognizing on the spot as "germs" . . . There had been but ten words, yet I had recognized in them, as in a flash, all the possibilities of the little drama of my *Spoils*.' The lady at the dinner party is not identifiable: the owner of 'Poynton' in the novel is known to have been drawn from Harriette (Mrs Frederick) Morrell.

[2] Newbolt goes on to analyse the differences between his own and James's treatment of the same theme — that of 'passing back from the life of to-day to scenes and actions in the life of a past generation'.

There is no reason either to question Newbolt's conclusions or to suspect James of unoriginality. *The Sense of the Past* had been begun in 1900 — six years before the publication of *The Old Country* — but had been laid aside and was only resumed about the time of the meeting with Newbolt.

'Too Much to Say'

Apropos of literary inclination Lady Lonsdale, now Lady Something Else, asked Harry to come see her at a certain hour one day as she had something of great importance to consult him about. When H. arrived she told him that she wanted to write a book about Boucher and Watteau[1] and wanted him to tell her how to begin, to which H. replied — 'There is no difficulty in beginning; the trouble is to leave off!'

Alice James, 1891

I met Henry James twice. First in the office of Mr J. B. Pinker. I was amused in secret, because he was so exactly like the (quite good-humoured) caricatural imitations of him by H. G. Wells. But I was also deeply impressed, not to say intimidated. Although I was nearer fifty than forty I felt like a boy. He had great individuality. And there was his enormous artistic prestige, and his staggering technical skill in the manipulation of words. He asked me if I ever dictated. I said that I could dictate nothing but letters; that I had once dictated a chapter of a novel but that the awful results decided me never to try it again. He said I might yet come to it. (I never shall.) He said he knew just how I felt, and that he had felt the same but had got into the habit of dictation . . . He expressed stupefaction when I said that I knew nothing about the middle classes, and indicated that the next time he saw me he would have recovered from the stupefaction and the discussion might proceed.

Talking about the material for novels he maintained that there was too much to say about everything, and that was what was most felt by one such as himself, not entirely without — er — er — perceptions. When I told him that sometimes I lay awake at night thinking of the things I had forgotten to put into my novels, he said that my novels were 'crammed', and that when

---

[1] Lady Gladys Herbert married successively the Earls of Lonsdale and de Grey (later Marquis of Ripon). No book by her on Boucher of Watteau appears to be on record.

something was 'crammed' nothing else could be put in, and so it was all right.

Arnold Bennett

DICTATING

[James's habit of dictating cannot be dated with any assurance. For private letters it was something unusual for him, demanding apology, in 1897: to be more exact, he apologized for 'Remingtonese' at intervals for the rest of his life, but he seems to have begun doing so early in 1897. For novels, according to Percy Lubbock, the habit was confirmed in 1898. Several critics have seen in dictation a major influence behind the 'third manner'; but if to date the habit by some fancied change of style in a particular chapter of a particular book is critically smart it is not altogether safe.]

1885?

'You began,' I interposed . . . 'this method of composition by aid of amanuensis in the middle of *Princess Casamassima*?'
   'How did you know that?' he shot back . . .
   'Because,' I said, 'that is where your style began to change.'
   'Oh!' he mused, frowningly.

Robert Herrick

1896?

'I can tell you,' [Marion] Crawford said to James, 'exactly when you began to dictate — in such and such a chapter of *What Maisie Knew*.' Henry James admitted it.

Maud Howe Elliott

Ghost Story

'Do you know,' [said James of 'The Turn of the Screw',] 'I wrote that story with the intention of terrifying every reader, and in the course of its composition I thought it would be a total failure. I dictated every word of it to a Scot,[1] who never from first to last betrayed the slightest emotion, nor did he ever make any comment. I might have been dictating statistics. I would dictate some phrase that I thought was blood-curdling; he would quietly take this down, look up at me and in a dry voice say, "What next?" '

W. L. Phelps

Evidence of an Amanuensis

[Miss Bosanquet became James's secretary in 1907.]

He was as easy to spell from as an open dictionary. The experience of years had evidently taught him that it was not safe to leave any word of more than one syllable to luck. He took pains to pronounce every pronounceable letter, he always spelt out words which the ear might confuse with others, and he never left a single punctuation mark unuttered, except sometimes that necessary point, the full stop. Occasionally in a low 'aside' he would interject a few words for the enlightenment of the amanuensis, adding for instance, after spelling out *The Newcomes*, that the words were the title of a novel by Thackeray . . .

'I know,' he once said to me, 'that I'm too diffuse when I'm dictating.' But he found dictation not only an easier but a more inspiring method of composing than writing with his own hand, and he considered that the gain in expression more than compensated for any loss of concision. The spelling out of the words, the indication of commas, were scarcely felt as a drag on the movement of his thought. 'It all seems,' he once explained, 'to be so much more effectively and unceasingly *pulled* out of me in speech than in writing.' . . .

For full-length novels . . . with a clear run of 100,000 words or more before him, Henry James always cherished the delusive expectation of being able to fit his theme quite easily between the

---

[1] 'Mr McAlpine, who is Mr James's secretary . . . This young man is just the person to help Mr James. He has a bump of reverence and appreciates his position and opportunity.' — *Mrs James T. Fields*, 1898.

covers of a volume. It was not until he was more than half way through that the problem of space began to be embarrassing. At the beginning he had no questions of compression to attend to, and he 'broke ground', as he said, by talking to himself day by day about the characters and construction until the persons and their actions were vividly present to his inward eye. This soliloquy was of course recorded on the typewriter. He had from far back tended to dramatize all the material that life gave him, and he more and more prefigured his novels as staged performances, arranged in acts and scenes, with the characters making their observed entrances and exits. These scenes he worked out until he felt himself so thoroughly possessed of the action that he could begin on the dictation of the book itself — a process which has been incorrectly described by one critic as re-dictation from a rough draft. It was nothing of the kind . . . The preliminary sketch was seldom consulted after the novel began to take permanent shape, but the same method of 'talking out' was resorted to at difficult points of the narrative as it progressed, always for the sake of testing in advance the values of the persons involved in a given situation, so that their creator should ensure their right action both for the development of the drama and the truth of their relations to each other.

For the volumes of memories, *A Small Boy and Others, Notes of a Son and Brother* and the uncompleted *Middle Years*, no preliminary work was needed. A straight dive into the past brought to the surface treasure after treasure, a wealth of material which became embarrassing . . . It was extraordinarily easy for him to recover the past; he had always been sensitive to impressions and his mind was stored with records of exposure. All he had to do was to render his sense of those records as adequately as he could. Each morning, after reading over the pages written the day before, he would settle down in a chair for an hour or so of conscious effort. Then, lifted on a rising tide of inspiration, he would get up and pace up and down the room, sounding out the periods in tones of resonant assurance. At such times he was beyond reach of irrelevant sounds or sights. Hosts of cats — a tribe he usually routed with shouts of execration —

might wail outside the window, phalanxes of motor-cars bearing dreaded visitors might hoot at the door. He heard nothing of them. The only thing that could arrest his progress was the escape of the word he wanted to use. When that had vanished he broke off the rhythmic pacing and made his way to a chimney-piece or book-case tall enough to support his elbows while he rested his head in his hands and audibly pursued the fugitive.

Theodora Bosanquet

To be Read Aloud

Drawn off into a corner of the room by Henry James, I spoke of testing a written style by reading it aloud; that I had found many passages in Browning which seemed obscure to the eye were transparently clear when I read them aloud. To my surprise he became excited. With intense earnestness he whispered in my ear, 'I have never in my life written a sentence that I did not mean to be read aloud, that I did not specifically intend to meet that test; you try it and see.[1] Only don't you tell.'

W. L. Phelps

UNAPPRECIATED

[As early as 1888 James wrote to Howells that the demand for his books had been reduced to zero, and in 1893 to Stevenson, 'Tell it not in Samoa — or at least not in Tahiti; but I *don't* sell ten copies!' If these were exaggerations it is the fact that many of his later books did not go beyond

[1] Several critics — notably Desmond MacCarthy, Hugh Walpole and F. M. Hueffer — have independently urged upon readers who find James's 'third manner' difficult that they should read him aloud. 'Sentences which puzzle the eye,' writes MacCarthy, 'in spite of involutions and clauses, then become clear to ear.' Bernard Shaw, on the other hand, explaining James's failure as a playwright has written: 'There is a literary language which is perfectly intelligible to the eye yet utterly unintelligible to the ear even when it is easily speakable by the mouth. Of that English James was a master in the library and a slave on the stage.' According to Shaw certain passages in one of the plays contained no word of more than two syllables, were word for word as simple as *The Pilgrim's Progress* but ' "came across" as gibberish'.

a first impression during his life-time, while the collected Novels and Tales over which he lavished great care was a costly failure. He is quoted above on page 39 as having said to Desmond MacCarthy in about 1899, 'My books make no more sound or ripple now than if I dropped them one after the other into the mud.']

He alluded gratefully to my letters of appreciation of his stories. 'I have for many years discharged my books into America as into a hollow void,' he admitted with sombre inflection; 'no word but yours has lately come back to me.'

Hamlin Garland

It would give me great pleasure that you should dedicate a book[1] to me — if you should see your way, in your own 'interest', to doing anything so inauspicious as to invoke my presence in respect to the popularity of the outcome. May my name, I mean, contribute to bring your work better fortune than it usually contributes to bring mine.

H. J. to G. Atherton, 1904

One night I was dining at the Garrick with W. W. Jacobs and at an adjoining table a friend was entertaining Max Beerbohm and Henry James. After dinner Jacobs and I went to their table for coffee, and I introduced Jacobs, whom Henry had never met. We sat and talked; suddenly James leant across and said, 'Mr Jacobs, I envy you.' 'You, Henry James, envy me!' cried Jacobs, always the most modest of men. James acknowledged the compliment with a graceful wave of the hand. 'Ah, Mr Jacobs,' he said, 'you are popular! Your admirable work is appreciated by a wide circle of readers; it has achieved popularity. Mine — never goes into a second edition. I should so much have loved to be popular!'

Alfred Sutro

[1] *The Bell in the Fog*, 1905, in the name-story of which the hero is drawn from James.

PORTRAIT BY ARTHUR BENSON

First Meetings

It was a hot Sunday in the July of 1884, soon after I had taken my
degree . . . I went to luncheon with Fred Myers [in Cambridge,
and there saw] a small, pale, noticeable man, with a short,
pointed beard and with large, piercingly observant eyes. He was
elegantly dressed in a light grey suit, with a frock coat of the same
material, and in the open air he wore a white tall hat. His name
was mentioned and it transported me with delight — Mr Henry
James. I knew some of his books well; indeed my father had
quoted *Roderick Hudson* shortly before in a University
sermon — 'my ecclesiastical passport', as Henry James said smil-
ingly to me — and he was one of my chief literary heroes. He
talked little and epigrammatically. He had not yet acquired, or he
did not display, that fine conversational manner of his later
years, which I shall try hereafter to describe.[1] . . . I recollect a
dim consciousness at the time that the attention of Henry James
was bent indulgently and benignantly upon me, that he was definitely concerned with me, extracting from me the data, so to
speak, of a little personal problem which he deigned to observe.
The sense of this was deeply and subtly flattering, combined as it
was with a far-reaching sort of goodwill.

He never lost touch with me from that hour. Two or three
meetings stand out prominently in my mind at subsequent dates.
I lunched with him at De Vere Gardens, and was called for after
luncheon by my mother, who came in. When we departed Henry
James, who was wearing a black velvet smoking-jacket with red
frogs, put on his tall hat and came down to the street. He suddenly became aware of his unaccustomed garb at the side of the

[1 See pages 36–7 above.]

carriage and hurriedly retreated to the shelter of the porch where he stood waving mute and intricate benedictions till we drove away. Again he came to stay with us at Addington [in the winter of 1895] after the collapse of one of his plays. He talked, I remember, to my mother and myself with great good-humour of the failure, and went on to speak of his other writing. He said that hitherto he seemed to himself to have been struggling in some dim water-world, bewildered and hampered by the crystal medium, and that he had suddenly got his head above the surface, with a new perspective and an unimpeded vision.[1] . . . He and my father on that occasion found much to say to each other. [Not long afterwards] he told me that it was on that visit that my father had told him a story which was the germ of that most tragical and even appalling story, 'The Turn of the Screw'.[2] My father took a certain interest in psychical matters, but we have never been able to recollect any story that he ever told which could have provided a hint for so grim a subject . . .

On another occasion [in June 1895] he came down to dine with me at Eton, when I had a boarding-house. He was to have stayed the night, but he excused himself on the score of illness; and when he appeared it was obvious that he was suffering: he was very pale, and had a gouty lameness which gave him much discomfort. But he talked energetically, and even came with me into the boys' passages to see two or three boys whose parents he knew. He limped distressfully but he was full of attention and observation. He commented admiringly on pictures and furniture, he asked the boys whimsical little questions, and heard them with serious discernment. He ought certainly to have been in bed; and I never saw so complete a triumph of courtesy and genuine interest over bodily pain.

Latterly I used to engage myself to dine or lunch in his company at the Athenaeum. You would see him enter, serious and

[1] ' "All my earlier work was subaqueous, subaqueous", he said. "Now I have got my head, such as it is, above the water, such as it was".' — *E. F. Benson.*

[2] Cf. H. J. to A. C. Benson, 11 March 1898 and *The Art of the Novel,* pages 169–70. Other origins of 'The Turn of the Screw' have been detected, notably by Robert Wolff who points out that Benson's recollection in the passage quoted above is not wholly accurate.

grave, with compressed lips — he was clean-shaven in the later years — breasting the air with a decisive and purposeful walk; and then he would catch sight of you and his eyes and lips would expand in a half-ironical and wholly indulgent smile — his mood was always indulgent. The meal itself was always a curious affair; he would get engaged in talk, look with absent-minded surprise at his food, and then, becoming aware that he was belated, take a few mouthfuls and send his plate away — it was impossible to persuade him to a leisurely consumption.

The Master at Home

[Rye, 17 January 1900] Henry James, looking somewhat cold, tired and old, met me at the station: most affectionate, patting me on the shoulder and really welcoming, with abundance of *petits soins* . . .

Dined simply at 7.30, with many apologies from H. J. about the fare . . . He was full of talk, though he looked weary, often passing his hand over his eyes; but he refined and defined, was intricate, magniloquent, rhetorical, humorous, not so much like a talker, but like a writer repeating his technical processes aloud — like a savant working out a problem. He told me a long story about——, and spoke with hatred of business and the monetary side of art. He evidently thinks that art is nearly dead among English writers — no criticism, no instinct for what is good . . .

He talked of Mrs Oliphant, Carlyle — whatever I began.

'I had not read a *line* that the poor woman had written for *years* — not for years; and when she died Henley — do you know him, the rude, boisterous, windy, headstrong Henley? — Henley, as I say, said to me, "Have you read *Kirsteen*?" I replied that as a matter of fact, no — h'm — I had not read it. Henley said, "That you should have any pretensions to interest in literature and should dare to say that you have not read *Kirsteen*!" I took my bludgeoning patiently and humbly, my dear Arthur — went back and read it, and was at once confirmed, after twenty pages, in my belief — I laboured through the book — that the poor soul had a simply *feminine* conception of literature: such slipshod, imperfect, halting, faltering, peeping, down-at-heel work — buffeting along like a ragged creature in a high wind, and just struggling to the goal, and falling in a quivering mass of faintness and fatuity. Yes, no doubt she was a gallant woman — though with no species of wisdom — but an artist, an artist—— !'

He held up his hands and stared woefully at me . . .

H. J. works hard; he establishes me in a little high-walled white parlour, very comfortable, but is full of fear that I am unhappy. He comes in, pokes the fire, presses a cigarette on me, puts his hands on my shoulder, looks inquiringly at me, and hurries away. His eyes are *piercing*. To see him, when I came down to breakfast this morning, in a kind of Holbein square cap of velvet and black velvet coat, scattering bread on the frozen lawn to the birds, was delightful . . .

We lunched together with his secretary, a young Scot. H. J. ate little, rolled his eyes, waited on us, walked about, talked — finally hurried me off for a stroll before my train. All his instincts are of a kind that make me feel vulgar — his consideration, hospitality, care of arrangement, thoughtfulness . . . He seemed to know everyone to speak to — an elderly clergyman in a pony-carriage, a young man riding. Three nice-looking girls met us, two of fourteen and fifteen, and a little maid of seven or eight, who threw herself upon H. J. with cooing noises of delight and kissed him repeatedly and effusively, the dogs also bounding up to him. He introduced me with great gravity . . . We got to the station; he said an affectionate farewell, pressing me to come again; I went away refreshed, stimulated, sobered.

Athenaeum Encounters

[London, 29 April 1904] I took H. J. to a secluded seat [in the smoking-room at the Athenaeum] and we had a talk . . . I questioned him about his ways of work. He admitted that he worked *every* day, dictated every morning, and began a new book the instant the old one was finished. He said it was his only chance because he worked so slowly and excised so much. I asked him when the inception and design of a *new* book was formed; and he gave no satisfactory answer to this except to roll his eyes, to wave his hand about, to pat my knee and to say, 'It's all *about*, it's about — it's in the air — it, so to speak, follows me and dogs me.'

Then Hardy came up and sat down the other side of me. I make it a rule *never* to introduce myself to the notice of distinguished men unless they recognize me; Hardy had looked at me, then looked away, suffused by a misty smile, and I presently gathered that this was a recognition — he seemed hurt by my not speaking to him . . . Then we had an odd triangular talk. Hardy could not hear what H. J. said, nor H. J. what Hardy said; and I had to try and keep the ball going. I felt like Alice between the two Queens. Hardy talked rather interestingly of Newman . . . He said very firmly that N. was no logician; that the *Apologia* was simply a poet's work, with a kind of lattice-work of logic in places to screen the poetry. We talked of Maxime Du Camp and Flaubert, and H. J. delivered himself very oracularly on the latter. Then Hardy went away wearily and kindly.

Then H. J. and I talked of Howard's *Belchamber*.[1] H. J. said it was a good idea, a good situation.

'He kindly read it to me; and we approached the dénouement in a pleasant Thackerayan manner — and then it was suddenly all at an end. He had had his chance and he has made *nothing* of it! Good Heavens, I said to myself, he has made nothing of it! I tried, with a thousand subterfuges and doublings, such as one uses with the work of a friend, to indicate this. I hinted that the *interest* of the situation was not the *experiences* — which were dull and shabby and disagreeable enough in all conscience, and not disguised by the aristocratic atmosphere — not the *experiences*, but the *effect* of the fall of wave after disastrous wave upon Sainty's *soul* — if one can use the expression for such a spark of quality as was inside the poor rat — that was the interest, and I said to myself, "Good God, why this chronicle, if it is a mere passage, a mere antechamber, and leads to nothing?" '

I think I have got this marvellous tirade nearly correct.

[8 November 1911] Went to Athenaeum. Then Henry James

---

[1] For what James wrote to Howard Sturgis about *Belchamber* see his letter to Sturgis, 8 November 1903. Edith Wharton attributed to James's criticism the discouragement which led Sturgis to give up writing novels.

appeared, looking stout and well, and rather excitedly cheerful. He would not talk but hurried off to order his dinner . . . He returned at 7.30 and we sat down together. There is something about him which was not there before, something stony, strained, anxious. But he was deeply affectionate and talked very characteristically. He said of P.'s article on William Morris that it was charming but began at the wrong end — that it was a well-combed, well-dressed figure, and that P. had overlooked the bloody, lusty, noisy *grotesque* elements in Morris. 'In these things, my dear Arthur, we must always be *bloody*.' . . . He had read Arnold Bennett.

'The fact is that I am so *saturated* with impressions that I can't take in new ones. I have lived my life, I have worked out my little conceptions, I have an idea how it all ought to be done — and here comes a man with his great voluminous books, dripping with detail — but with no scheme, no conception of character, no *subject* — perhaps a vague idea of just sketching a character or two — and then comes this great panorama, everything perceived, nothing seen *into*, nothing related. He's not afraid of masses and crowds and figures — but one asks oneself what is it all for, where does it all tend, what's the *aim* of it?'

By this time we had dawdled and pecked through our dinner — he ate a hearty meal, and there was much of that delicious gesture, the upturned eye, the clenched upheld hand, and that jolly laughter that begins in the middle of a sentence and permeates it all . . .

Then he spoke about Hugh Walpole — he said he was charming in his zest for experience and his love of intimacies. 'I often think,' he went on, 'if I look back at my own starved past, that I wish I had done more, reached out further, claimed more — and I should be the last to block the way. The only thing is to be there, to wait, to sympathize, to help if necessary.' . . . He joined all this with many pats and caressing gestures; then led me down by the arm and sent me off with a blessing. I felt he was glad that I should go — had felt the strain — but that he was well and happy. He is a wonderful person, so entirely simple in emotion and loyalty, so complicated in mind. His little round head, his fine gestures, even to the waiters — 'I am not taking any of this — I don't need this' — his rolling eyes, with the heavy lines round them, his rolling resolute gait, as if he *shouldered* something and set off with his burden — all very impressive.

[18 April 1914] Back to the Athenaeum and fell in with Henry James, very portly and gracious — a real delight. I had tea with him and he talked very richly . . . He complimented me grotesquely and effusively as likely to incur the jealousy of the gods for my success and efficiency. He little knows! My books are derided, my activities are small and fussy. I said this, and he smiled benignantly.

I asked him if he was well. He said solemnly that he lived (touching his heart) with a troublesome companion, angina pectoris. 'But you look well.' He laughed — 'I *look*, my dear Arthur, I admit I *look* — but at that point I can accompany you no further. It's a look, I allow.' And so we said good-bye; he shook my hands often very affectionately.

[21 April 1915] I lunched with Henry James who kept on being entangled by voluble persons . . . H. J. was very tremendous; he looks ill, he changes colour, he is dark under the eyes — but he was in a cheerful and pontifical mood. He ate a plentiful meal of veal and pudding but he spoke to me very gravely of his physical condition and his chronic angina . . . We went down together and he made a most affectionate farewell. He is slower and more *soigneux* in utterance than ever, but leaves a deep impression of majesty, beauty and greatness. He said that his life was now one flurried escape from sociability.

Final Benediction

The last time that I saw him he was lunching at the Athenaeum, and I went up to him — he had a companion — and said that I only came for a passing benediction. He put his hand on my arm and said: 'My dear Arthur, my mind is so constantly and continuously bent upon you in wonder and goodwill that any change in my attitude could be only the withholding of a perpetual and settled felicitation.' He uttered his little determined, triumphant laugh, and I saw him no more.

A. C. Benson[1]

---

[1] The dated paragraphs above are from Benson's diary, kept at the time. The first and last sections are from an essay written after James's death.

LAMB HOUSE

[In the summer of 1896 James took first Reginald Blomfield's cottage at Playden and then 'a frumpy, shabby, practically gardenless parsonage' in Rye. He was much drawn to the Sussex countryside, to the town of Rye and, in Rye, to 'the mansion with the garden house perched on the wall' — Lamb House. This early eighteenth-century house at the top of the town he first took on a 21-year lease in September 1897 and later bought. From 1898 until his death he spent nearly all his summers and a few winters there.]

AMERICAN VISITORS

From New England

[Mrs Fields, widow of the Boston publisher, and Sarah Orne Jewett, the New England short-story writer, were among the earliest visitors to Lamb House.]

We left London about 11 o'clock for Rye, to pass the day with Mr Henry James. He was waiting for us at the station with a carriage, and in five minutes we found ourselves at the top of a silent little winding street, at a green door with a brass knocker, wearing the air of impenetrable respectability which is so well known in England. Another instant and an old servant, Smith (who with his wife has been in Mr James's service for 20 years), opened the door and helped us from the carriage. It was a pretty interior — large enough for elegance and simple enough to suit the severe taste of a scholar and private gentleman.

Mr James was intent on the largest hospitality. We were asked upstairs over a staircase with a pretty balustrade and plain green drugget on the steps; everything was of the severest plainness,

but in the best taste — 'not at all austere', as he himself wrote us
. . . [Downstairs] we sat in the parlour opening on a pretty
garden for some time, until Mr James said he could not conceive
why luncheon was not ready and he must go and inquire, which
he did in a very responsible manner, and soon after Smith
appeared to announce the feast. Again a pretty room and table.
We enjoyed our talk together sincerely at luncheon and afterward strolled into the garden. The dominating note was dear Mr
James's pleasure in having a home of his own to which he might
ask us.

From the garden of course we could see the pretty old house
still more satisfactorily. An old brick wall concealed by vines and
laurels surrounds the whole irregular domain; a door from the
garden leads into a paved courtyard which seemed to give Mr
James peculiar satisfaction; returning to the garden, and on the
other side, at an angle with the house, is a building which he
laughingly called the temple of the Muse. This is his own place
par excellence. A good writing-table and one for his secretary, a
typewriter, books and a sketch by du Maurier, with a few other
pictures (rather mementoes than works of art), excellent windows
with clear light — such is the temple! Evidently an admirable spot
for his work[1] . . .

[After sight-seeing at Winchelsea] Mr James drove us to the
station, where we took the train for Hastings. He had brought his
small dog, an aged black-and-tan terrier, with him for a holiday.
He put on the muzzle, which all dogs just now must wear, and
took if off a great many times until, having left it once when he
went to buy the tickets and recovered it, he again lost it and it
could not be found; so as soon as he reached Hastings he took a
carriage again to drive us along the esplanade, but the first thing
was to buy a new muzzle . . . We began to feel like tea, so . . . we
went into a small shop and enjoyed more talk under new conditions. 'How many cakes have you eaten?' 'Ten,' gravely replied
Mr James — at which we all laughed. 'Oh, I know,' said the girl
with a wise look at the desk. 'How do you suppose they know?'

[1] This temple of the Muse was demolished on 18 August 1940 by a bomb which
also did some damage to the structure of Lamb House.

said Mr James musingly as he turned away. 'They always do!'
And so on again presently to the train.

Mrs James T. Fields, 1898

From the Middle West

After our tea, which was served on a little table out under the
trees, he took me to see the town, pointing out the most ancient of
the buildings, well knowing that as a man from the plains of Iowa
I would be interested in age-worn walls and door-sills . . .

Everybody we met seemed to know and like him; whether they
recognized in him a famous author or not I cannot tell, but they
certainly regarded him as a good neighbour. He greeted everyone
we met most genially. He was on terms with the postman and the
butcher's boy. There was nothing austere or remote in his
bearing. On the contrary he had the air of a curate making the
rounds of his village . . . The people everywhere greeted him
with smiling cordiality. They liked and honoured him, that was
evident, and it gave me a keen sense of satisfaction to find him
more and more neighbourly, taking an interest in what his fellow
citizens were doing and thinking. This phase of him was as
surprising as it was amusing. To hear him asking after a child's
health, or inquiring when Mr Brown would return from London,
was a revelation of the fact that after all he was more than half
New England.[1]

Hamlin Garland

From New York

At Lamb House an anxious frugality was combined with the wish
that the usually solitary guest (there were never at most more
than two at a time) should not suffer too greatly from the contrast

---

[1] As first published in a magazine this paragraph ended: '. . . he was basically
more than half of New England blood.' This is a popular fallacy: Hueffer
described James as 'a New Englander *pur sang*'. In fact his ancestors were Scots
and Irish, settled since the eighteenth century in New York State and New Jersey.

between his or her supposed habits of luxury and the privations imposed by the host's conviction that he was on the brink of ruin. If any one in a pecuniary difficulty appealed to James for help he gave it without counting; but in his daily life he was haunted by the spectre of impoverishment.[1] . . . He lived in terror of being thought rich, worldly or luxurious, and was for ever contrasting his visitors' supposed opulence and self-indulgence with his own hermit-like asceticism, and apologizing for his poor food while he trembled lest it should be thought too good. I have often since wondered if he did not find our visits more of a burden than a pleasure, and if the hospitality he so conscientiously offered and we so carelessly enjoyed did not give him more sleepless nights than happy days.

I hope not; for some of my richest hours were spent under his roof. From the moment when I turned the corner of the grass-grown street mounting steeply between squat brick houses, and caught sight at its upper end of the wide Palladian window of the garden-room, a sense of joyous liberation bore me on. There *he* stood on the doorstep, the white-panelled hall with its old prints and crowded book-cases forming a background to his heavy loosely-clothed figure. Arms outstretched, lips and eyes twinkling, he came down to the car, uttering cries of mock amazement and mock humility at the undeserved honour of my visit. The arrival at Lamb House was an almost ritual performance, from those first ejaculations to the large hug and the two solemn kisses executed in the middle of the hall rug. Then, arm in arm, through the oak-panelled morning-room we wandered out on to the thin worn turf of the garden, with its ancient mulberry tree, its unkempt flower-borders, the gables of Watchbell Street peeping like village gossips over the creeper-clad walls and the scent of roses spiced with a strong smell of the sea. Up and down the lawn we strolled with many pauses, exchanging news, answering each other's questions, delivering messages from the other members of the group, inspecting the strawberries and lettuces in the tiny

---

[1] 'He now lives on river at Chelsea. He likes pavements, shop-fronts and the convenient taxi. He said, "If I was rich, instead of being in grovelling poverty . . ." ' — *Arnold Bennett*, 1914.

kitchen-garden and the chrysanthemums 'coming along' in pots in the greenhouse; till at length the parlour-maid appeared with a tea-tray and I was led up the rickety outside steps to the garden-room, that stately and unexpected appendage to the unadorned cube of the house . . .

At Lamb House my host and I usually kept to ourselves until luncheon. Our working hours were the same, and it was only now and then that we went out before one o'clock to take a look at the green peas in the kitchen-garden or to stroll down the High Street to the Post-Office. But as soon as luncheon was dispatched (amid unnecessary apologies for its meagreness and sarcastic allusions to my own supposed culinary extravagances) the real business of the day began. Henry James, an indifferent walker and incurably sedentary in his habits, had a passion for motoring . . . Everything pleased him — the easy locomotion (which often cradled him into a brief nap), the bosky softness of the landscape, the discovery of towns and villages hitherto beyond his range, the magic of ancient names, quaint or impressive, crabbed or melodious. These he would murmur over and over to himself in a low chant, finally creating characters to fit them, and sometimes whole families with their domestic complications and matrimonial alliances, such as the Dymmes of Dymchurch, one of whom married a Sparkle and was the mother of little Scintilla Dymme-Sparkle, subject of much mirth and many anecdotes. Except during his naps nothing escaped him, and I suppose no one ever felt more imaginatively, or with deeper poetic emotion, the beauty of sea and sky, the serenities of the landscape, the sober charm of villages, manor-houses and humble churches, and all the implications of that much-storied corner of England.

One perfect afternoon we spent at Bodiam — my first visit there. It was still the old spell-bound ruin, unrestored, guarded by great trees and by a network of lanes which baffled the invading charabancs. Tranquil white clouds hung above it in a windless sky, and the silence and solitude were complete as we sat looking across at the crumbling towers, and at their reflection in a moat starred with water-lilies and danced over by great blue dragon-flies. For a long time no one spoke; then James turned to me and said solemnly: 'Summer afternoon — summer afternoon; to me those have always been the two most beautiful words in the English language.'

Edith Wharton

Uninvited

Americans, with or without introductions, would sometimes break in on his working hours. 'My devastating countrymen' he called them, and used to tell us about them afterwards. But he was actually most forbearing, much as he might curse them subsequently in his quaint manner.

A. G. Bradley

DISTINGUISHED NEIGHBOURS

W. J. Seeks Chesterton

I once saw James quarrelling with his brother William James, the psychologist. He had lost his calm; he was terribly unnerved. He appealed to me, to me of all people, to adjudicate on what was and what was not permissible behaviour in England. William was arguing about it in an indisputably American accent, with an indecently naked reasonableness. I had come to Rye with a car to fetch William James and his daughter to my home at Sandgate. William had none of Henry's passionate regard for the polish upon the surfaces of life and he was immensely excited by the fact that in the little Rye inn, which had its garden just over the high brick wall of the garden of Lamb House, G. K. Chesterton was staying. William James had corresponded with our vast contemporary and he sorely wanted to see him. So with a scandalous directness he had put the gardener's ladder against that ripe red wall and clambered up and peeped over! Henry had caught him at it.

It was the sort of thing that isn't done. It was most emphatically the sort of thing that isn't done . . . Henry had instructed the gardener to put away that ladder and William was looking thoroughly naughty about it. To Henry's manifest relief I carried William off and in the road just outside the town we ran against the Chestertons . . . William got his coveted impression.

H. G. Wells

H. J. Finds Belloc

One summer we took a house at Rye . . . It happened that the house next to us was the old oak-panelled mansion which had attracted, one might almost say across the Atlantic, the fine aquiline eye, of Henry James . . . [Mr H. G. Wells used] to make irreverent darts and dashes through the sombre house and the sacred garden and drop notes to me over the garden wall . . . Mr Henry James heard of our arrival in Rye and proceeded (after exactly the correct interval) to pay his call in state.

Needless to say, it was a very stately call of state; and James seemed to fill worthily the formal frock-coat of those far-off days. As no man is so dreadfully well-dressed as a well-dressed American, so no man is so terribly well-mannered as a well-mannered American. He brought his brother William with him, the famous American philosopher; and though William James was breezier than his brother when you knew him, there was something finally ceremonial about this idea of the whole family on the march. We talked about the best literature of the day; James a little tactfully, myself a little nervously . . . He said something complimentary about something of mine; but represented himself as respectfully wondering how I wrote all I did. I suspected him of meaning why rather than how. We then proceeded to consider gravely the work of Hugh Walpole, with many delicate degrees of appreciation and doubt; when I heard from the front garden a loud bellowing noise resembling that of an impatient fog-horn. I knew however that it was not a fog-horn; because it was roaring out, 'Gilbert! Gilbert!' . . . I knew it was Belloc, probably shouting for bacon and beer; but even I had no notion of the form or guise under which he would present himself.

I had every reason to believe that he was a hundred miles away in France. And so apparently he had been; walking with a friend of his in the Foreign Office, a co-religionist of one of the old Catholic families; and by some miscalculation they had found themselves in the middle of their travels entirely without money . . . Their clothes collapsed and they managed to get into some workmen's slops. They had no razors and could not afford a shave. They must have saved their last penny to re-cross the sea; and then they started walking from Dover to Rye; where they knew their nearest friend for the moment resided. They arrived, roaring for food and drink and derisively accusing each other of having secretly washed, in violation of an implied contract between tramps. In this fashion they burst in upon the balanced tea-cup and tentative sentence of Mr Henry James.

Henry James had a name for being subtle; but I think that situation was too subtle for him. I doubt to this day whether he, of all men, did not miss the irony of the best comedy in which he ever played a part. He left America because he loved Europe, and all that was meant by England or France; the gentry, the gallantry, the traditions of lineage and locality, the life that had been lived beneath old portraits in oak-panelled rooms. And there, on the other side of the tea-table, was Europe, was the old thing that made France and England, the posterity of the English squires and the French soldiers; ragged, unshaven, shouting for beer, shameless above all shades of poverty and wealth; sprawling, indifferent, secure. And what looked across at it was still the Puritan refinement of Boston; and the space it looked across was wider than the Atlantic.

G. K. Chesterton

WORKROOMS

Since winter was approaching, Henry James had begun to use a panelled, green-painted room on the upper floor of Lamb House for his work. It was known simply as the green room. It had many advantages as a winter workroom, for it was small enough to be easily warmed and a wide south window caught all the morning sunshine. The window overhung the smooth green lawn, shaded in summer by a mulberry tree, surrounded by roses and enclosed behind a tall brick wall. It never failed to give the owner pleasure to look out of this convenient window at his English garden where he could watch his English gardener digging the flower-beds or mowing the lawn or sweeping up fallen leaves. There was another window for the afternoon sun, looking towards Winchelsea and doubly glazed against the force of the westerly gales. Three high bookcases, two big writing-desks and an easy chair filled most of the space in the green room, but left enough clear floor for a restricted amount of the pacing exercise that was indispensable to literary composition.

On summer days Henry James liked better to work in the large 'garden-room' which gave him a longer stretch for perambulation and a window overlooking the cobbled street that curved up the hill past his door. He liked to be able to relieve the tension of a difficult sentence by a glance down the street; he enjoyed hailing a passing friend or watching a motor-car pant up the sharp little slope. The sight of one of these vehicles could be counted on to draw from him a vigorous outburst of amazement, admiration or horror for the complications of an age that produced such efficient monsters for gobbling up protective distance.

Theodora Bosanquet

[James's voice dictating in the garden-room] boomed out through the open window between the tassels of the wistaria, now louder, now softer, as he paced up and down the length of the room and the metallic click of the typewriter made response. From breakfast until the stroke of the gong for lunch he was thus invisible though not inaudible: then there came a day when, though the morning was still only half-spent, he emerged from the inviolable precinct, and taking me by the arm he walked me about the lawn and involved himself in a noble harangue. To me, he said, fresh from the roar and reverberation of London with its multifarious movements and intensive interests, the news he was about to impart might reasonably seem to be of little moment, but to him in his quiet and red-walled *angulus terrae*, his little plot in Rye, that which had in fact happened this morning, and which was the cause of his indulging himself now with a mulberry at this unusual hour . . . On and on went the magnificent architectural period, and then, I suppose, not having the typist to read it out to him and thus give him a clue through the labyrinth, he confessed himself lost and added, 'In fact, my dear Fred Benson, I have finished my book.'

E. F. Benson

DOMESTIC CARES

Fire!

[Edward Warren, 'a very distingué architect and loyal spirit', was a close friend of James's and was responsible for the alterations and improvements at Lamb House in 1897–8. James's 72-word telegram to him on 27 February 1899 announcing the fire appears, together with an account of the occurrence to another correspondent, in *Letters*. The following extract is taken from John Russell's 'Henry James and his Architect'.]

I sat up late writing letters — in the green room . . . and towards 1.30, after an odour had long puzzled me, I found smoke coming up through the boards of the floor, near the fireplace. I roused Smith, got a pry, an axe — que sais-je? — and getting portions of the planks up, found *fire* under and behind the hearth and 'stove'. We rushed for police and fire brigade, and they arrived with very decent promptness and operated with intelligence and tact. The inflamed material — morsels of *beams* going under the 'stove', which has been nobly hot for six weeks — as well as other compromised and compromising elements dropped (while the men tore away fireplace, grate, tiles, hearth, brickwork and all, leaving a gaping void) down into the *pocket* beside the flue of the dining-room chimney, and there began (inside, naturally) to burn the dining-room walls. So a great square cavity had to be pickaxed from the dining-room in the portion above the mantel, through which the burning portion, which was not large but very active, was got at and quenched and extracted. Voilà! The brave pumpers departed with the early dawn. But I was sickened by the little desolation and defacement — the house befouled and topsy-turvy — and couldn't sleep.

H. J. to E. Warren, 1899

Servants

It was at my cottage, Point Hill as it is called, that Henry James made the acquaintance of Rye. He took it in the months when we were not there, and was here year after year, tended by a devoted manservant whom we used to call Bardolph, after that rascal in Shakespeare whose 'nose would light a torch in hell'. Bardolph was devoted to his master and was much exercised about his health, because Henry James in those days used to go out on this bicycle and return in a state of complete deliquescence, for he was no athlete and quite unused to any form of active exercise; indeed later on, when he had bought Lamb House, it was his custom to take the train to Hastings in the afternoons in order to get exercise by walking up and down the nice paved promenade.

Reginald Blomfield

['Bardolph' was the Smith mentioned by Mrs Fields on page 173 above. In 1901 when, James wrote, they had been in his service for sixteen years Smith and his wife were 'sacrificed to the just gods' — 'shot into space (thank heaven at last!) by a whirlwind of but 48 hours duration'. According to F. M. Hueffer all the female servants had left in a body on account of the 'carryings-on' of the butler. It is characteristic of Hueffer's romancing that he should have credited the Smiths with *thirty* years in James's service — which would place their engagement by him some five years before he came to live in England.

Hueffer, as the next extract shows, exaggerated also when he credited Lamb House with seven servants — 'housekeeper, butler, upper house-

maid, lower housemaid, tweeny maid, knife-boy, gardener'. James was
about to let the house for six months.]

I make the house over to you, practically, just as I have been
living in it, and you will find it, I make bold to say, in very good
and tidy condition. I leave all the Servants, who amount to five in
number, including the Gardener and the Houseboy. The latter
has his meals in the house, but doesn't sleep, and the Gardener of
course does neither, having his cottage close by the garden gate.
You will find this functionary, George Gammon, an excellent,
quiet, trustworthy fellow in all respects — a very good carpenter
into the bargain and thoroughly handy at mending anything that
gets broken in the house. I have endowed him with a small hand-
cart, which is kept in the vault beneath the Garden-room, highly
convenient to the House door, and which I find quite sufficient
for the conveyance of my luggage, or that of visitors, to and from
the Station for all comings and goings. The distance is so short
that it means, save in some extraordinary rain, the complete
suppression of flies — which is a great simplification.

The Cook-Housekeeper, Mrs Paddington, is really, to my
sense, a pearl of price: being an extremely good cook, an absolutely brilliant economist, a person of the greatest order, method
and respectability, and a very nice woman generally. If you will,
when you let her see you each morning, in the dining-room after
breakfast, just also suffer her to take you into the confidence, a
little, of her triumphs of thrift and her master-strokes of manage-
ment, you will get on with her beautifully — all the more that she
gets on beautifully with her fellow-servants, a thing that all 'good'
cooks don't do. . .

The Parlour-maid, Alice Skinner, has lived with me for six
years — that is with an interval of no great length — and is a
thoroughly repectable, well-disposed, and duly competent
young woman. And the Housemaid is very pretty and gentle —
and not a very, *very* bad one. The House-boy, Burgess Noakes,
isn't very pretty, but is on the other hand very gentle, punctual
and desirous to please — and has been with me three years . . .
[Besides other duties] he brushes clothes and 'calls', in the
morning, those of his own sex who may repose beneath the roof.

Lastly, though of such diminutive stature,[1] he is, I believe, nineteen years old.

The Servants will of course tell you just what tradesmen I employ, and I should be glad if you could go on with the same. They are in fact the inevitable ones of the place, and are all very decent, zealous, reasonable folk. I leave almost everything 'out' save some books, of a certain rarity and value, which I lock up; and there is, I think, a full sufficiency of forks and spoons etc., as well as of all household linen.

Lastly I take the liberty of confiding to your charity and humanity the precious little person of my Dachshund Max, who is the best and gentlest and most reasonable and well-mannered, as well as most beautiful, small animal of his kind to be easily come across — so that I think you will speedily find yourselves loving him for his own sweet sake. The Servants, who are very fond of him and good to him, know what he 'has', and when he has it; and I shall take it kindly if he be not too often gratified with tid-bits between meals. Of course what he most intensely dreams of is being taken out on walks, and the more you are able so to indulge him the more he will adore you and the more all the latent beauty of his nature will come out. He is, I am happy to say, and has been from the first (he is about a year and a half old) in very good, plain, straightforward health, and if he is not overfed, and is sufficiently exercised, and adequately brushed (his brush being always in one of the bowls on the hall-table — a convenient little currycomb) and Burgess is allowed occasionally to wash him, I have no doubt he will remain very fit.

H. J. to Louise Horstmann, 1904

He was waited upon by two or three faithful servants. Foremost among them was the valet and factotum, Burgess, always spoken

[1] Burgess, says A. G. Bradley, was about five feet high and an enthusiastic lightweight boxer. James took him to America in 1910 and described him to Henry White, whom master and man were about to visit, as 'so diminutive that he takes up little room, but also so athletic that he yearns to make himself generally useful; in short an intensely modest pearl'.

of by his employer as 'poor little Burgess'. Burgess's broad squat figure and phlegmatic countenance are a familiar memory to all who frequented Lamb House, and James's friends gratefully recall his devotion to his master during the last unhappy years of nervous break-down and illness. He had been preceded by a man-servant whom I did not know, but of whom James spoke with regard as an excellent fellow. 'The only trouble was that when I gave him an order he had to go through three successive mental processes before he could understand what I was saying. First he had to register the fact that he was being spoken to, then to assimilate the meaning of the order given to him, and lastly to think out what practical consequences might be expected to follow if he obeyed it.'

Perhaps these mental gymnastics were excusable in the circumstances; but Burgess apparently soon learned to dispense with them, and without any outward appearance of having understood what his master was saying carried out his instructions with stolid exactitude. Stolidity was his most marked characteristic. He seldom gave any sign of comprehension when spoken to, and I remember once saying to my Alsatian maid, who was always as quick as a flash at the uptake: 'Do you know, I think Burgess must be very stupid. When I speak to him I'm never even sure that he's heard what I've said.' My maid looked at me gravely. 'Oh, no, Madam: Burgess is remarkably intelligent. *He always understands what Mr James says.*' And that argument was certainly conclusive.

Edith Wharton

RYE SOCIETY

Tea-Parties

Rye society consisted in his day of perhaps a score of households, besides others in the neighbourhood, a few literary or artistic, the majority just 'retired' gentle-folk, civil or military, with the local parsons, doctors and lawyers. Henry James was no recluse: he was fond of his fellow-creatures — after three p.m., till which hour his privacy was sacrosanct. He attended Rye tea-parties freely, had beautiful manners and no aversion to local gossip, which was of course in his favour.

His talk over the tea table was generally quite light and human, but always whimsical. He had no trace of American accent. Indeed his diction was ultra-fastidious, like that of the older University dons. There was more than a touch of his books in his talk, when he would raise his hand and half close his eyes in quest of exactly the right word, which, when found, not seldom brought a twinkle into his eyes as he met yours. For the gesture had a half-conscious touch of humour in it.

He was always very nice to me, partly because I had written a good many books, though they were not the sort he read — when he read anything — and also because I was the only person in the locality who knew America as a former resident and understood his personal and local allusions. Not that he was partial to his countrymen in general. The tone in which he pronounced the words 'Middle West' was worth hearing. Of the South, my particular section, he had no personal knowledge and no great opinion — 'a provincial people' and, in his sense, quite uncultured . . .

Touring sketching classes sometimes filled the narrow streets and crowded on to his doorstep, all unconscious of the distinguished occupant, because it commanded a popular view. H. J. used to declare that on these occasions he couldn't get out of his house without 'taking a flying leap over the heads of art and industry' — the vision of his stout unathletic frame and short legs in the air being his little joke.

A. G. Bradley

He was a kind-hearted and sympathetic man, full of consideration for others, modest and even diffident considering his great and well-deserved reputation, and yet conscious of what was due to him. He once remarked to me on the occasion of an entertainment at Rye, at which in his opinion undue attention had been paid to a person of title, that it was 'a deplorable evening in every way'.

Reginald Blomfield

Dress

He thought that for every social occasion a correct costume could be prescribed and a correct behaviour defined. On the table (an excellent piece) in his hall at Rye lay a number of caps and hats, each with its appropriate gloves and sticks; a tweed cap and a stout stick for the marsh, a soft comfortable deerstalker if he were to turn aside to the golf club, a light-brown felt hat and a cane for a morning walk down to the harbour, a grey felt with a black band and a gold-headed cane of greater importance if afternoon calling in the town was afoot.

H. G. Wells

Golf Club

Henry James chose Rye as a residence because, he declared, he liked golfers in plus-fours.

Ella Hepworth Dixon

Henry James's description of golf as 'a princely expenditure of time' is well worth recording.

C. C. H. Millar

One afternoon I played golf at Camber . . . He met us after our game at the club-house and gave us tea, in an ecstasy of genial nebulosity as to what we had been doing. 'Some beflagged jam pots, I understand, my dear Fred, let into the soil at long but varying distances. A swoop, a swing, a flourish of steel, a dormy': and he wrote to Arthur saying that he thought I put golf too high among intellectual pursuits.

E. F. Benson

Till his years advanced I used often to take country walks with him. He loved the quiet English landscape, but characteristically had not the faintest knowledge of the rural industries that went to the making of the picture. He was a subscribing member of our famous Rye golf club. But he would have been the first to make merry at the idea of his swinging a club. Occasionally, however, after a walk on the shore he would look in at the club for tea and be greeted with a shout by any friends present. His fine mobile face would then light up as with characteristic elaboration he delivered some humorous repartee in the Jamesian fashion . . .

The unabashed Philistine who cares for nothing but sport and fancies himself on that account alone, a fairly common type in England, was a real puzzle to Henry James. He sometimes cited a certain prosperous neighbour as a luminous example of this, to him, bewildering type. When taken by his wife to Rome for the first time and asked what he thought of it, he replied, 'Nothing at all. It has the worst golf course in Europe.' This gave H. J. huge delight.

A. G. Bradley

I have heard the secretary of a golf club, a dour silent man who never addressed five words to myself though I was one of his members, talk for twenty minutes to the Master about a new bunker that he was thinking of making at the fourteenth hole. And James never touched a niblick in his life.

F. M. Hueffer

Cricket Week

During our annual cricket weeks at Rye he used to come on to the ground, but he always used to sit in the tent talking to the ladies with his back to the cricket, probably thinking the game too absurd to be worth the attention of serious people.

Reginald Blomfield

1914–1916

THE WAR

[Soon after the outbreak of war in August 1914 James moved from Rye to London. The failure of the United States to join the Allies became a source of great and growing bitterness to him. His first war work was a pamphlet on the American Volunteer Motor Ambulance Corps (of whose London committee he was chairman); almost his last was an article on the Belgian refugees, whose arrival in Rye he had witnessed in September 1914 and to whose welfare in a Chelsea recreation centre he lent his energy for many months. Both pamphlet and article were designed to enlist American subscribers, but neither of them — nor yet another article intended for the New York *Tribune* on 'the British soldier, his aspect, temper and tone . . . as I have seen him since the begining of the war in Hospital', nor another on the insulation of the Briton — did he succeed in 'placing' in what was still, till the summer of 1915, his own country. In England:]

To all who listened to him in those days it must have seemed that he gave us what we lacked — a voice; there was a trumpet note in it that was heard nowhere else and that alone rose to the height of the truth.

Percy Lubbock

August 1914

Quite in the beginning of August 1914 he said to two English friends, 'However British you may be, I am more British still.'

Edmund Gosse

The German Judas

I met him at a lunch in August [1914] when the veil of the Temple
was metaphorically rent from top to bottom. He had been invited
by an American, but far from tactful, hostess to meet some von
Bülows who had been caught in London, or rather abandoned by
the German Embassy in its hurried flight.

Conversation was dancing upon perilous ice. The hostess
insisted on bringing it to the subject of Belgian atrocities, in which
she declined to believe. Henry James subsided into a napkin! But
worse was to come. She began praising the Kaiser, who amongst
many superb gestures by land and sea had once condescended to
board her yacht. She had had the honour to peel a pear for
him! — he could not do it so very well with his injured arm,
etc.!

At this Henry James emerged from his napkin like a ruddy
volcano under its frail cap of snow, thrust his chair back, called
the whole lunch party to order and, in one long, ominous, speed-
gathering, hysterical, overwhelming, objurgatory sentence, condemned that unfortunate but now forgotten Emperor to comparisons rather in favour of Judas Iscariot.

It was like a thunderbolt falling from the blue of a Watteau
picnic. Nobody dared rise. Nobody dared leave. The lunch was
very good and I only remember that we finished it in deadly
silence and that no faces bore such looks of anguished fear as the
von Bülows, who felt they had been trapped!

Shane Leslie

The Moral Position

Old Henry James asked me to come and see him and was extraordinarily affectionate, kissing me on both cheeks when I arrived
and thanking me enormously for coming. He is passionately English and says it is almost good that we were so little prepared, as it
makes our moral position so splendid. He almost wept as he
spoke. He says America is enthusiastically with us, both from

sympathy of ideas and obvious interest, and that the Bernsdorff
campaign has ludicrously failed.

John Bailey, October 1914

Mr Page

Pinker had also seen Henry James, who often goes to see [Walter
H.] Page, American Ambassador, in afternoons. They have long
quiet talks together. First time H. J. opened his heart to Page he
stopped and said: 'But I oughtn't to talk like this to you, a neutral.' Said Page: 'My dear man, if you knew how it does me good
to hear it!' Hy. James is strongly pro-English and comes to
weeping-point sometimes.

Arnold Bennett, November 1914

Nothing but the War[1]

Henry James, gouty, dyspeptic, short-sighted, could do
nothing — but he did that magnificently! He had moved into a
flat in Chelsea, started a brougham, and entertained the British
Army in the widest sense of the word. Drawing-rooms interested
him no longer. He now talked Army, thought Army, and died
Army — quite suddenly.

I shall never forget his rage when I told him of how Mrs Fisher
(Adrienne Dairolles), who had played for him in *Guy Domville*[2]
had been lunching with some ladies of the English upper classes
who were doing all sorts of war work, and doing it very nicely
too. They were bragging of 'our men' at Ypres, justly enough, but
one of them, less British than the others, had sufficient detachment to observe the angry dismay of a Frenchwoman whose
countrymen were being quite unconsciously left out of this

---

[1] These paragraphs represent five pages of *The Flurried Years*, shortened by
excisions (which are not indicated) and by the substitution of an occasional
sentence or phrase from a briefer account of the same subject contributed by
Violet Hunt to the *Daily Mail* of 1 March 1916.

[2] Adrienne Dairolles played in *The American* but not in *Guy Domville*.

paean. With the high courtesy of her race, and it is to be feared some of its stupidity, she put in a word for Mrs Fisher's benefit, saying with a note of flippant patronage, 'And the *French* did very well, *too!'* He boiled. I boiled. We boiled together.

The uses of his sympathy naturally fell to the country of his adoption — 'Anything I can do, anything I can write!' No war appeal went unregarded; he even allowed himself to be interviewed. The chaste Henry! Words were put into his mouth — ineptitudes! Greater love hath no man than [that] he lay down his *style* for his friend. He was so willing to help that he was eager to be comprehended of the people.

Mary Robinson asked him to write an article for the *Book of France*. He said to me, shyly: 'I want you to let me read you something I have written. Perhaps you would be kind enough to tell me if I am comprehensible? They tell me' — he turned his head away — 'that I am obscure.' A pause. He was preparing apologies for the immense compliment he was going to pay me. 'You must not think that I am preparing to experiment on a vile body — yours. I just remembered that you were one of my oldest friends.'

He read, standing, walking up and down in the front part of the room a long way from where I sat. But I heard. His voice, strong, resonant — the wonderful voice that old invalid men can muster when put to it — trembled, not from feebleness but from emotion. I was stirred beyond measure and I exclaimed, impertinent on a wave of enthusiasm which earned my pardon, 'Mr James! I did not know you could be so — *passionate*!'

He had risen and was walking shyly away from me towards a bookcase. He turned on me an eye, *narquois*, reflective, storklike, a little devilish, calmly wise, and with a little pompous laugh — 'Ah, madam, you must not forget that in this article I am addressing — not a Woman, but a Nation!'

Of course he had gout now, like any good old English gentleman. Sometimes he would have his foot — both feet — swathed in linen bandages, laid out helplessly on a chair in front of him — 'My old pain in possession' — very much annoyed if I dropped my glove or something that, however near his chair, he could not pick up for me. He would be a little untidy perhaps, dressing-gown unequally disposed over night-gear, looking what he was — a thoroughly ugly man, with eyes dull, dyspeptic and inward, flat and deep set, like land-locked bays, gloomy, relieved at times by the harbour-lights of humour — a stony twinkle of innocent malice.

But, well or ill, it was understood that we talked in these days of war and nothing but war. There was to be no resumption of the Society gossip in which he used to delight. It was what one had gathered about Zeppelin defences on the east coast, or whether one thought the recruiting good at Cardiff or at Redcar: were the streets nicely full of khaki? And what did soldiers back from the front tell you, and could you bring the tired officer to see him who, after the battle of the Marne, riding into Paris, had made a détour to see the Château de Pierrefonds? — he would wear him next his heart, for he loved to think of an officer as a Bayard who had not altogether lost his love of the arts. Rupert Brooke, a little wounded but able to come to lunch, he cherished like a son. He would never speak of Rupert Brooke after he had died.[1]

Violet Hunt

Colonel House

I will record here the last time but one that I ever saw Henry James — a vision, an impression, which the retina of memory will surely keep to the end. It was at Grosvenor Place in the autumn of 1915, the second year of the war. How doubly close by then he had grown to all our hearts! His passionate sympathy for England and France, his English naturalization — *a beau geste* indeed, but so sincere, so moving — the pity and wrath that carried him to sit by wounded soldiers and made him put all literary work aside as something not worth doing, so that he might spend time and thought on helping the American ambulance in France — one must supply all this as the background of the scene.

[1] Perhaps. But he wrote of him: James's last completed work was his preface to Brooke's *Letters from America* (published 1916): a simpler and more spontaneous memorial will be found in James's letters to Edward Marsh, 6 and 13 June 1915.

It was a Sunday afternoon. Our London house had been let for a time, but we were in it again for a few weeks, drawn into the rushing tide of war-talk and war anxieties. The room was full when Henry James came in. I saw that he was in a stirred, excited mood, and the key to it was soon found. He began to repeat the conversation of an American envoy to Berlin — a well-known man — to whom he had just been listening. He described first the envoy's impression of the German leaders, political and military, of Berlin. 'They seemed to him like men waiting in a room from which the air is being slowly exhausted. They *know* they can't win! It is only a question of how long, and how much damage they can do.' The American further reported that after his formal business had been done with the Prussian Foreign Minister, the Prussian, relaxing his whole attitude and offering a cigarette, said, 'Now then let me talk to you frankly, as man to man!' and began a bitter attack on the attitude of President Wilson. Colonel [House] listened, and when the outburst was done, said, 'Very well! Then I too will speak frankly. I have known President Wilson for many years. He is a very strong man, physically and morally. You can neither frighten him nor bluff him.' And then — springing up in his seat — 'And, by Heaven, if you want war with America you can have it to-morrow!'

Mr James's dramatic repetition of this story, his eyes on fire, his hand striking the arm of his chair, remains with me as my last sight of him in a typical representative moment.

Mrs Humphry Ward

Hospital Visitor

[Lady Lyttelton] told me a fine thing — how he went to a hospital last year where there was a man who had lost both legs at the Front and had no more hope or wish for life, so that they thought he would die. But dear old Henry went to him and said in such a moving way: 'Dear man, be proud and happy; try to think how all who see you all your life will envy and admire you — how you are beginning a new and wonderful life from having been able to

make this tremendous and supreme offering to the greatest cause
that ever men fought for.' The man was so surprised and con-
quered that he became a new creature and got well.

John Bailey, 1916

NATURALIZATION

The Neutral

I was asked to meet Henry James at luncheon [at Mrs Wharton's
shortly after the outbreak of war], and into the room he burst, his
great eyes ablaze.

'My hands, I must wash them!' he cried. 'My hands are dripping with blood. All the way from Chelsea to Grosvenor Place I
have been bayoneting, my dear Edith, and hurling bombs and
ravishing and raping. It is my daydream to squat down with King
George of England, with the President of the French Republic and
the Czar of Russia on the Emperor William's belly, until we
squeeze out of it the last irrevocable drops of bitter retribution.'

Mrs Wharton, who had come over in a blaze from Paris, said
that she must have a seat with the others. 'No, Edith,' was the
stern reply of this august septuagenarian. 'That imperial stomach
is no seat for ladies. This is a war for men only: it is a war for me
and poor Logan.'

'But surely we must discriminate,' I mildly suggested to this
master of discriminations; 'surely we must look to the right and
left, and proceed, all eyes, with care and strategical caution. This
is certainly my war, as I am a naturalized British subject; but you,
I believe, are a neutral, as neutral as Switzerland or Sweden. Why
don't you come into it?' I asked him as, panting, he paused to
wipe the imagined gore from his face, 'why don't you enrol
yourself as a British subject?'

More than once during the winter that followed I would end
with this trumpet-note my colloquies with Henry James on the
telephone. 'When are you coming into the war?' I would hiss;

'how long are you going to sit with the Roumanians on a back seat in the Balkans?'

One day the elaborations of phrase, the parentheses, the polysyllabic evasions, which made a talk on the telephone with Henry James so amazing an adventure, were replaced by a terse query.

'Logan, how — you know what I mean — how do you do it?'

'You go,' I tersely replied, 'to a solicitor.'

'Of course. I know just the right person': and this great man of action rang off with a bang that must almost have smashed the receiver.

Logan Pearsall Smith

Sponsors

[The decision was taken in June 1915, and as sponsors James secured the Prime Minister Mr Asquith, George Prothero, Edmund Gosse and J. B. Pinker. His letter to Asquith is printed in the latter's *Memories and Reflections*.]

[Asquith] was delighted to become one of the sponsors who had formally to vouch for the eligibility to British citizenship of this distinguished American and personal friend, but added that 'the bonds of friendship were strained to cracking when I had to subscribe to the proposition that he could both talk and write English'.

Life of H. H. Asquith

Declaration of Faith

We are able to announce that Mr Henry James was granted papers of naturalization on Monday [26 July] and took the oath of allegiance as a British subject . . . The reasons which Mr James gives in his petition [are]: —

Because of his having lived and worked in England for the best part of forty years; because of his attachment to the country and his sympathy with it and its people; because of the long friendships and associations and interests he has formed here — these last including the acquisition of some property: all of which things have brought to a head his desire to throw his moral weight and personal allegiance, for whatever they may be worth, into the scale of the contending nation's present and future fortune.

The Times, 28 July 1915

'Why, Mr James, precisely, did you do it?'

He answered, 'My dear Purple Patch, chiefly because I wanted to be able to say *We* — with a capital — when I talked about an Advance.'[1]

Violet Hunt

LAST ILLNESS

[On 2 December 1915 James had a stroke. After a second stroke some days later he did not again leave his bed.]

We all knew that for years he had suffered from the evil effects of a dangerous dietary system, called (after the name of its egregious inventor) 'Fletcherizing'. The system resulted in intestinal atrophy, and when a doctor at last persuaded him to return to a normal way of eating he could no longer digest, and his nervous system had been undermined by years of malnutrition. The Fletcher fad, moreover, had bred others, as usually happens; and James's incessant preoccupation with his health gradually led to periods of nervous depression. The death of his brother William shook him to the soul, not only because of their deep attachment to each other, but because Henry, following the phases of his brother's fatal malady, had become convinced that he had the same organic heart-disease as William . . .

His dying was slow and harrowing. The final stroke had been preceded by one or two premonitory ones, each causing a

---

[1] In the first week of the war he had written to his nephew, 'You see how I talk of "we" and "our" — which is so absolutely instinctive and irresistible with me that I should feel quite abject if I didn't!'

diminution just marked enough for the still conscious intelligence to register it, and the sense of disintegration must have been tragically intensified to a man like James, who had so often and deeply pondered on it, so intently watched for its first symptoms. He is said to have told his old friend Lady Prothero, when she saw him after the first stroke, that in the very act of falling (he was dressing at the time) he heard in the room a voice which was distinctly, it seemed, not his own, saying: 'So here it is at last, the distinguished thing!'

Edith Wharton

ORDER OF MERIT

When [James] became naturalized . . . Mr Asquith told me he was thinking of recommending him for the Order of Merit. . . . A little later he said he was doubtful whether he could bring it off, as John Morley was opposed to it; but he asked me to write him a minute in support. What Lord Morley's reasons precisely were I never knew; but I gathered that the novels did not appeal to him because they dealt too exclusively with the inconsequential doings of the Idle Rich, and were therefore not what the Americans would call 'worth while'[1] . . . However that may be, I set to work and produced what I thought a cogent plea.

Edward Marsh

The King has been graciously pleased to make the following appointment to the Order of Merit: —

HENRY JAMES, ESQ.

[1] Thirty-eight years earlier Morley, as literary adviser to Macmillans, had reported on *French Poets and Novelists* (the second of James's books to be published in England and the first of a long series over the Macmillan imprint): 'Of charm, delicacy, finesse [the essays] have none . . . I feel that the book might have some slight sale, but it would certainly make no deep literary mark. There would be no harm in printing it, but neither to literature would there be any good . . . It is honest scribble work and no more.'

Mr Henry James recently became naturalized in this country to mark his sympathy with the cause of the Allies. The high honour now conferred on him will give the keenest satisfaction to lovers of literature all over the world . . . He joins Mr Hardy in the Order, membership of which is the highest distinction attainable by a writer, and in which they are the only two representatives of pure literature.

The Times, 1 January 1916

[The insignia of the Order were taken to his bedside by Lord Bryce. The story that follows, like that of the first stroke on page 198, has been variously told, always, so far as is known, at second or third hand.]

Sir Edmund Gosse, one of his closest friends, himself told me this charming story about it. He had asked leave to tell Henry James of the award, but on entering the sick-room he found his friend lying with closed eyes in the flickering light of a single candle, and the nurse told him she was afraid the patient was past hearing anything. Leaning over the bed Gosse whispered, 'Henry, they've given you the O. M.,' but not a sign of interest shewed in the still face, and Gosse quietly left the room. Directly the door closed Henry James opened his eyes and said, 'Nurse, take away the candle and spare my blushes.'

J. S. Bain

DEATH

[James died on 28 February 1916. His body was cremated. The Dean of Westminster and the Prime Minister agreed that the funeral service might be held in the Abbey, but it was held, on 3 March, in Chelsea Old Church.]

[12 March] Called on Mrs William James. She said Henry James had ordered a very simple religious service only at Golder's Green, but she felt that he had not understood how many of his friends would wish to come, [so she] had decided on the service at the Old Chelsea Church where he used occasionally to drop in and where he liked to remember Sir Thos. More had sung in the choir.

John Bailey, 1916

[On the south wall of the More Chapel in Chelsea Old Church, since destroyed by a bomb, was erected a memorial tablet:]

In memory of Henry James O. M., Novelist: born in New York 1843: died in Chelsea 1916: lover and interpreter of the fine amenities, of brave decisions and generous loyalties: a resident of this parish who renounced a cherished citizenship to give his allegiance to England in the first year of the Great War.

LIST OF SOURCES

Unless otherwise stated, the place of book publication is London

Abbey, E. A. *Edwin Austin Abbey, The Record of his Life and Work*, by E. V. Lucas, 2 vols. (1921).

Adams, H. *Letters of Henry Adams, 1858–1891*, edited by Worthington Chauncey Ford (1930).

Adams, Mrs H. *The Letters of Mrs Henry Adams, 1865–1883*, edited by Ward Thoron (1937).

Allingham, William. *A Diary*, edited by H. Allingham and D. Radford (1907).

Anstey, F. (Thomas Anstey Guthrie). *A Long Retrospect* (Oxford, 1936).

Archer, William. Theatrical criticisms signed 'W. A.' *The World*, 7 January, 30 September and 18 November 1891.

——*The Theatrical 'World' of 1895* (1896).

——*William Archer, Life, Work and Friendships*, by Lieut.-Col. C. Archer (1931).

Asquith, H. H. See Oxford and Asquith, Earl of.

Atherton, Gertrude. *Adventures of a Novelist* (1932).

Bailey, John. *Letters and Diaries*, edited by his wife (1935).

Bain, James S. *A Bookseller Looks Back* (1940).

Barrie, J. M. *The Greenwood Hat* (1937).

Barzun, Jacques. 'James the Melodramatist', *The Kenyon Review*, Henry James number, Autumn 1943.

Beer, Thomas. *Stephen Crane* (1924).

Benedict, Clare. *The Benedicts Abroad* (1930).

Bennett, Arnold. *Things that have Interested Me* (1921).

——*The Journals of Arnold Bennett*, edited by Newman Flower, 3 vols. (1932–3).

Benson, A. C. *Memories and Friends* (1924).

——*The Diary of Arthur Christopher Benson*, edited by Percy Lubbock (1926).

Benson, E. F. *Our Family Affairs, 1867–1896* (1920).

——*As We Were* (1930).

——*Final Edition* (1940).

——See also James, Henry. *Letters to A. C. Benson, etc.*

Blanche, Jacques-Emile. *Mes Modèles* (Paris, 1928).

——*Portraits of a Lifetime*, translated and edited by Walter Clement (1937).

Blathwayt, Raymond. *Looking Down the Years* (1935).

Blomfield, Sir Reginald. *Memoirs of an Architect* (1932).

Boit, Louise. 'Henry James as Landlord,' *Atlantic Monthly*, August 1946.

Bosanquet, Theodora. *Henry James at Work* (1924).

Boughton, Alice. 'A Note by his Photographer', *Hound and Horn*, Henry James number, April-May 1934.

Bradley, A. G. 'Henry James as I Knew Him', *John o' London's Weekly*, 18 December 1936.

Brookfield, Arthur Montagu. *Annals of a Chequered Life* (1930).

Carr, Mrs J. Comyns. *Reminiscences*, edited by Eve Adam (1926).

Charteris, Evan. *John Sargent* (1927).

Chesterton, G. K. *Autobiography* (1936).

Conrad, Jessie. *Joseph Conrad as I Knew Him* (1926).

Daly, Joseph Francis. *The Life of Augustin Daly* (New York, 1917).

Daudet, Madame Alphonse. *Notes sur Londres, mai 1895* (Paris, 1897).

Daudet, Léon. *L'Entre-deux-guerres*, Souvenirs, 3° série (Paris, 1915).

Dixon, Ella Hepworth. *As I Knew Them* (1930).

Draper, Muriel. *Music at Midnight* (1929).

Edel, Léon. *Henry James, Les années dramatiques* (Paris, 1931).

Elliot, W. G. *In My Anecdotage* (1925).

Elliott, Maud Howe. *My Cousin, F. Marion Crawford* (1934).

Field, Michael. *Works and Days*, edited by T. and D. C. Sturge Moore (1933).

Flaubert, Gustave. *Correspondance*, VIIe série (Paris, 1930).

Forbes-Robertson, Sir Johnston. *A Player under Three Reigns* (1925).

Ford, Ford Madox. See Hueffer, F. M.

Garland, Hamlin. *Roadside Meetings* (1931).

Godley, A. D. *Reliquiae*, edited by C. R. L. Fletcher, 2 vols. (Oxford, 1926).

Gosse, Edmund. 'The Funeral of Henry James,' *The ·Times*, 4 March 1916.

——*Aspects and Impressions* (1922).

——*The Life and Letters of Sir Edmund Gosse*, by Evan Charteris (1931).

Guedalla, Philip. *Supers and Supermen* (1920).

Hardy, T. *The Early Life of Thomas Hardy, 1840-1891*. Compiled by Florence Emily Hardy (1928).

——*The Later Years of Thomas Hardy, 1892-1928*, by Florence Emily Hardy (1930).

Hay, J. *The Life and Letters of John Hay*, by William Roscoe Thayer, 2 vols. (1915).

Henderson, Archibald. *Bernard Shaw, Playboy and Prophet* (1932).

Herrick, Robert. 'A Visit to Henry James', *The Yale Review*, July 1923.

Hind, C. Lewis. *Naphtali* (1926).

Howe, M. A. De Wolfe. *Memories of a Hostess* (Mrs James T. Fields) (1923).

Howells, W. D. *Life in Letters of William Dean Howells*, edited by Mildred Howells, 2 vols. (1928).

Hueffer, Ford Madox. *Thus to Revisit* (1921).

——*Return to Yesterday*, by Ford Madox Ford (1931).

——*It was the Nightingale*, by Ford Madox Ford (1934).

——*Mightier than the Sword*, by Ford Madox Ford (1938). (U S title *Portraits from Life*.)

Hunt, Violet. *The Flurried Years* (1926).

——'The Last Days of Henry James', *Daily Mail*, 1 March 1916.

Hyndman, Henry Mayers. *Further Reminiscences* (1912).

James, Alice. *Alice James, Her Brothers: Her Journal*, edited by Anna Robeson Burr (1934).

James, Henry. *A Small Boy and Others* (1913).

——*Notes of a Son and Brother* (1914).

——*The Middle Years* (1917).

——*The Letters of Henry James*, selected and edited by Percy Lubbock, 2 vols. (1920).

——'Three Unpublished Letters and a Monologue', *The London Mercury*, September 1922.

——*Henry James: Letters to A. C. Benson and Auguste Monod*, edited by E. F. Benson (1930).

——*The Art of the Novel, Critical Prefaces*, introduction by Richard P. Blackmur (New York, 1935). A reprint in one volume of the eighteen prefaces in the New York edition of *The Novels and Tales of Henry James*, 24 vols. (1908–9).

James, William. *The Letters of William James*, edited by his son Henry James, 2 vols. (1920).

Jennings, Richard. 'Fair Comment.', *The Nineteenth Century*, May 1943.

Jordan, Elizabeth. *Three Rousing Cheers* (1938).

——'Henry James at Dinner', *Mark Twain Quarterly*, Henry James number, Spring 1943.

Leslie, Shane. 'A Note on Henry James', *Horizon*, June 1943.

Lowndes, Mrs Belloc. *The Merry Wives of Westminster* (1946).

Lubbock, Percy. *Mary Cholmondeley* (1928).

Lucas, E. V. *The Colvins and their Friends* (1928).

——*Reading, Writing and Remembering* (1932).

MacCarthy, Desmond. *Portraits, I* (1931).

——*Experience* (1935).

MacColl, D. S. *Life, Work and Setting of Philip Wilson Steer* (1945).

Mackenzie, Compton. 'Henry James', *Life and Letters To-day*, December 1943.

Marsh, Edward. *A Number of People* (1939).

Mason, A. E. W. *Sir George Alexander and the St James's Theatre* (1935).

Millar, C. C. Hoyer. *George du Maurier and Others* (1937).

Mills, J. Saxon. *Sir Edward Cook* (1921).

Moore, George. *Avowals* (1924).

Morgan, Charles. *The House of Macmillan, 1843–1943* (1943).

Nadal, E. S. 'Personal Recollections of Henry James', *Scribner's Magazine*, July 1920.

Newbolt, H. *The Later Life and Letters of Sir Henry Newbolt*, edited by Margaret Newbolt (1942).

Norton, C. E. *Letters of Charles Eliot Norton*, edited by Sara Norton and M. A. De Wolfe Howe, 2 vols. (1913).

O'Connor, Mrs T. P. *I Myself* (1910).

Oxford and Asquith, Earl of. *Memories and Reflections, 1852–1927*, 2 vols. (1928).

——*Life of Herbert Henry Asquith, Lord Oxford and Asquith*, by J. A. Spender and Cyril Asquith, 2 vols. (1932).

Pennell, Joseph. *The Adventures of an Illustrator* (1925).

——*The Life and Letters of Joseph Pennell*, by Elizabeth Robins Pennell, 2 vols. (1930).

Perry, Bliss. *And Gladly Teach* (Boston, 1935).

Perry, Ralph Barton. *The Thought and Character of William James*, 2 vols. (Oxford, 1935).

Phelps, William Lyon. *Autobiography with Letters* (Oxford, 1939).

Reid, Forrest. *Private Road* (1940).

Robertson, W. Graham. *Time Was* (1931) (U S title *Life was Worth Living*.)

Robins, Elizabeth. *Theatre and Friendship, Some Henry James Letters* (1932).

Rothenstein, William. *Men and Memories, 1872–1922*, 2 vols. (1931–2).

Russell, G. W. E. 'Talk and Talkers of To-day' (unsigned), *The New Review*, August 1889.

Russell, John. 'Henry James and his Architect', *The Architectural Review*, March 1943.

Sarawak, Ranee Margaret of. *Good Morning and Good Night* (1934).

Sassoon, Siegfried. *The Weald of Youth* (1942).

Scott, Clement. '*Guy Domville* at the St James's Theatre' (unsigned), *Daily Telegraph*, 7 January 1895.

Shaw, G. Bernard. *Dramatic Opinions and Essays*, 2 vols. (1907).

——'Mr Shaw on Printed Plays', the *Times Literary Supplement*, 17 May 1923.

Sichel, Walter. *The Sands of Time* (1923).

Smalley, George W. *Anglo-American Memories* (1911).

Smith, Logan Pearsall. 'Robert Bridges, Recollections.', *S P E Tract No. 35* (Oxford, 1931).

——*Unforgotten Years* (1938).

——'Saved from the Salvage.', *Horizon*, March 1943.

——'Slices of Cake', *New Statesman*, 5 June 1943.

Smyth, Ethel. *Impressions that Remained*, 2 vols. (1919).

——*What Happened Next* (1940).

Spender, Stephen. *The Destructive Element* (1935).

Sturgis, Howard Overing. *Belchamber*, introduction by Gerard Hopkins (Oxford, 1935).

Sutro, Alfred. *Celebrities and Simple Souls* (1933).

Symons, Arthur. '*The American* at the Opéra Comique', *The Academy*, 3 October 1891.

Times, The. Issues of 28 September 1891, 7 January 1895, 28 July 1915, 1 January 1916, 22 August 1930.

Walbrook, H. M. 'Henry James and the English Theatre', *The Nineteenth Century*, July 1916.

——'Henry James and the Theatre', *The London Mercury*, October 1929.

——*A Playgoer's Wanderings* (1926).

Walpole, Hugh. *The Aple Trees* (1932).

——'Henry James, A Reminiscence', *Horizon*, February 1940.

Ward, Geneviève, and Richard Whiteing. *Both Sides of the Curtain* (1918).

Ward, Mrs Humphry. *A Writer's Recollections* (1918).

——*The Life of Mrs Humphry Ward*, by Janet Penrose Trevelyan (1923).

Waterlow, S. P. 'Memories of Henry James', *New Statesman*, 6 February 1926.

Wells, H. G. *Boon . . .* 'Prepared for publication by Reginald Bliss. With an ambiguous introduction by H. G. Wells' (1915).

——*Experiment in Autobiography*, 2 vols. (1934).

Westminster Gazette, The. Issues of 9 and 10 January 1895.

Wharton, Edith. *A Backward Glance* (1934).

——*The House of Mirth*, with a new introduction (Oxford, 1936).

Whitall, James. *English Years* (1936).

White, H. *Henry White, Thirty Years of American Diplomacy* by Allan Nevins (New York, 1930).

Wilde, Oscar. *Selected Works*, edited by Richard Aldington (1946).

Wolff, Robert. 'The Genesis of *The Turn of the Screw*', *American Literature*, March 1941.

Woolf, Virginia. *Roger Fry* (1940).

ACKNOWLEDGEMENTS

The letters of Henry James quoted in this book from various published and unpublished sources appear by courtesy of Mr Henry James, of New York, the novelist's nephew. The compiler would acknowledge a special debt of gratitude to Mr James.

The list of sources on pages 202–6 records all the books and articles which have been drawn upon, whether for extracts quoted verbatim in the body of this volume or for information used in the introduction, editorial comments and footnotes. For permission to quote extracts acknowledgements are due to the following publishers, authors and others:—

George Allen & Unwin Ltd. (*Looking Down the Years* by Raymond Blathwayt, *Mightier than the Sword* by Ford Madox Ford); Appleton-Century Company (*Bernard Shaw* by Archibald Henderson); Appleton-Century Company and Mrs Royall Tyler (*A Backward Glance* by Edith Wharton); Ernest Benn Ltd. (*Memories of a Hostess* by M. A. De Wolfe Howe); Jonathan Cape Ltd. (*Adventures of a Novelist* by Gertrude Atherton, *Mary Cholmondeley* by Percy Lubbock, *Theatre and Friendship* by Elizabeth Robins, *The Destructive Element* by Stephen Spender); Jonathan Cape Ltd. and Harcourt Brace & Company Inc., New York (*English Years* by James Whitall); Cassell & Company Ltd. and Dr Philip Gosse (*Aspects and Impressions* by Edmund Gosse); Cassell & Company and the executors of the late C. C. Hoyer Millar (*George du Maurier and Others*); Cassell & Company and the Public Trustee (*The Journals of Arnold Bennett*); W. Collins Sons & Company Ltd. (*A Writer's Recollections* by Mrs Humphry Ward); Constable & Company Ltd. (*Letters of Henry Adams* edited by W. C. Ford, *Sir Edward Cook* by J. Saxon Mills, *Unforgotten Years* by Logan Pearsall Smith); Peter Davies Ltd. (*The Greenwood Hat* by J. M. Barrie); J. M. Dent & Sons Ltd. and Coward-McCann Inc., New York (*Portraits of a Lifetime* by Jacques-Emile Blanche); Gerald Duckworth & Company Ltd. (*Celebrities and Simple Souls* by Alfred Sutro); Faber and Faber Ltd. (*Life of Philip Wilson Steer* by D. S. MacColl, *Private Road* by Forrest Reid, *Men and Memories* by William Rothenstein, *The Weald of Youth* by Siegfried Sassoon); Faber & Faber Ltd. and the executors of the Newbolt estate (*Later Life and Letters of Sir Henry Newbolt*); the Golden Cockerel Press and the executors of the late Sir Hugh Walpole (*The Apple Trees*); Victor Gollancz

Ltd. and Mrs Janice Ford Biala (*Return to Yesterday* by Ford Madox Ford); Victor Gollancz Ltd. and the late H. G. Wells (*Experiment in Autobiography*); Editions Bernard Grasset, Paris (*L'Entre-deux-guerres* by Léon Daudet); Hamish Hamilton Ltd. (*Time Was* by W. Graham Robertson); Harper & Brothers, New York (*Henry White* by Allan Nevins); William Heinemann Ltd. (*Stephen Crane* by Thomas Beer, *Sir Edmund Gosse* and *John Sargent* by Evan Charteris, *Joseph Conrad as I Knew Him* by Jessie Conrad, *Music at Midnight* by Muriel Draper, *A Number of People* by Edward Marsh); William Heinemann Ltd. and Mr C. D. Medley (*Avowals* by George Moore); the Hogarth Press (*Henry James at Work* by Theodora Bosanquet, *Roger Fry* by Virginia Woolf); Houghton Mifflin Company, Boston, Mass. (*And Gladly Teach* by Bliss Perry); Hurst & Blackett Ltd. and the literary executor of the late Violet Hunt (*The Flurried Years*); Hutchinson & Company (Publishers) Ltd. (*Reminiscences* by Mrs J. Comyns Carr, *As I Knew Them* by Ella Hepworth Dixon); Hutchinson & Company and the executrix of the late G. K. Chesterton (*Autobiography*); Hutchinson & Company and Sir Maurice Bonham-Carter (*Life of H. H. Asquith* by J. A. Spender and Cyril Asquith); Hutchinson & Company and Mr K. S. P. McDowall (*Dairy of A. C. Benson* edited by Percy Lubbock); Miss Elizabeth Jordan (*Three Rousing Cheers*); John Lane the Bodley Head Ltd. (*Roadside Meetings* by Hamlin Garland); Little Brown & Company, Boston, Mass. (*Life and Letters of Joseph Pennell* by E. R. Pennell); Longmans Green & Company Ltd. (*As We Were* by E. F. Benson, *Impressions that Remained* by Ethel Smyth); Longmans Green & Company and Mr K. S. P. McDowall (*Final Edition* by E. F. Benson); Longmans Green & Company, Little Brown & Company and the Atlantic Monthly Press, and Mrs Ward Thoron (*Letters of Mrs Henry Adams* edited by Ward Thoron); Macmillan & Company Ltd. (*A Diary* by William Allingham, *A Bookseller Looks Back* by J. S. Bain, *Memoirs of an Architect* by Reginald Blomfield, *My Cousin F. Marion Crawford* by Maud Howe Elliott, *Further Reminiscences* by H. M. Hyndman, *Sir George Alexander and the St James's Theatre* by A. E. W. Mason, *The House of Macmillan* by Charles Morgan); Macmillan & Company and the executors of the Hardy estate (*The Early Life* and the *Later Years of Thomas Hardy* by Florence Emily Hardy); Macmillan & Company and the trustees of the James estate (*The Letters of Henry James* edited by Percy Lubbock); Macmillan & Company and Dodd, Mead & Company, New York (*Alice James, Her Brothers and Her Journal*); Methuen & Company Ltd. (*Edwin Austin Abbey* and *The Colvins and their Friends* by E. V.

Lucas); M. G.-A. Mévil-Blanche (*Mes Modèles* by J.-E. Blanche); John Murray (the *Letters and Diaries* of John Bailey, *Memories and Friends* by A. C. Benson, *Annals of a Chequered Life* by A. M. Brookfield, *Works and Days* by Michael Field); the Oxford University Press and the executors of the late Thomas Anstey Guthrie (*A Long Retrospect*); the Oxford University Press and Mrs Royall Tyler (Introduction to the World's Classics edition of *The House of Mirth* by Edith Wharton); the Oxford University Press, New York (*Autobiography with Letters* by W. L. Phelps); the Public Trustee, on behalf of the estate of Arnold Bennett (*Things that have Interested Me*); Putnam & Company Ltd. (*Portraits and Experience* by Desmond MacCarthy, *I Myself* by Mrs T. P. O'Connor); Charles Scribner's Sons Ltd. (*The Art of the Novel* by Henry James); George Bernard Shaw (*Dramatic Opinions*).

The *Atlantic Monthly* Company, Boston, Mass., and Mrs John Boit ('Henry James as Landlord'); the editor of *Horizon* and Sir Shane Leslie ('A Note on Henry James'); the editor of *Horizon* and the executors of the late Sir Hugh Walpole ('Henry James, a Reminiscence'); the editor of *Hound and Horn* ('A Note by his Photographer' by Alice Boughton); the editor of *John O'London's Weekly* ('Henry James as I Knew Him' by A. G. Bradley); the editor of *Life and Letters To-day* and Mr Compton Mackenzie ('Henry James'); the editor of the *New Statesman and Nation* ('Slices of Cake' by Logan Pearsall Smith, 'Memories of Henry James' by Sir S. P. Waterlow); the editor of the *Nineteenth Century and After* and Constable & Company Ltd. ('Fair Comment' by Richard Jennings, 'Henry James and the English Theatre' by H. M. Walbrook); Charles Scribner's Sons Ltd. ('Personal Recollections of Henry James' by E. S. Nadal); the Times Publishing Company Ltd. (various extracts from *The Times*).

If through inadvertence or failure to trace the present proprietors any copyright material has been included without proper acknowledgement, apologies are offered to those concerned.

For leave to quote unpublished material, privately communicated, the compiler would express his gratitude to Miss Ruth Draper, Miss Olivia Garnett and Mr Henry Dwight Sedgwick. For information and assistance of various kinds he would thank Mr G. E. Bates (of Messrs. Constable & Company), Mr Donald G. Brien, Mr G. C. R. Brookes, Mr Leon Edel, Mr Gaillard Lapsley, Mr Percy Lubbock, Sir Edward Marsh, Mr John Russell, Mr Ellery Sedgwick, Mr Stephen Spender, Mr Allan Wade, Mr A. F. Wells and a number of correspondents who kindly replied to a letter in the *Times Literary Supplement*.

FURTHER READING

Edel, Leon. *The Life of Henry James*, 5 vols. (1953–72); revised in 2 vols. (1977).

James, Henry. *Letters*, edited by Leon Edel, 4 vols. (1974–84).

——*The Notebooks of Henry James*, edited by F. O. Matthiessen and Kenneth B. Murdock (New York, 1947; Chicago, 1981).

——*Selected Literary Criticism*, edited by Morris Shapira (1963; Cambridge, 1981).

Matthiessen, F. O. *The James Family* (New York, 1947).

Moore, Harry T. *Henry James and his World* (1974).

INDEX

I. *James's Works*

II. *James's Tastes, Attitudes, and Characteristics*

III. Persons